Good Night, My Son

A Treasure In Heaven

Written By

Esther F. Smucker

First edition - March 1995
Second edition - May 1995

Printed in the United States of America.

Library of Congress Number
95-67135

International Standard Book Number
1-883294-20-7

Published by
Olde Springfield Shoppe
10 West Main Street, P. O. Box 171
Elverson, PA 19520-0171

— *Contents* —

Acknowledgements iv

Foreword v

1. Good Night, My Son 1
2. Little Angels 4
3. Premonition 9
4. My Life and Love Was Full 13
5. "I'm Going to Heaven, Mom" 16
6. Love In Action 22
7. Teddy Bears In Time of Tragedy 28
8. Reflections At the Viewing 33
9. Our Loss Was His Gain 36
10. Difficulty In Parting 41
11. There's Danger on the Road 47
12. Facing Life Again 49
13. Struggling For Survival 53
14. Not Again! 55
15. The Christmas Spirit 58
16. Spring Always Follows Winter 61
17. A Letter From Heaven 67
18. One Year Later 70
19. The Boys Tell Their Stories
      In Their Own Words 74
20. My Husband Tells His Story 76
21. Trooper Bittner Shares His Story 81

— *Acknowledgements* —

Sometimes one need words of encouragement from friends to undertake a project or to complete a task. Sometimes it takes more than that; persistent urging may also be needed. This is especially true when it comes to writing something for the public to read.

I extend my appreciation to many friends who took an interest and had a part in preparing this book for publication.

· For **Debbie Walton** who convinced me that this story should be shared in hopes of benefiting others.

· For **Ernest and Naomi Zimmerman** whose constant encouragement and the use of their typewriter played a major role in preparing this story.

· For **Ira Wagler** who proofread the manuscript and corrected the grammatical errors. His input was of much value and appreciated by the author.

· For **John A. Hostetler** who recommended the manuscript to the publisher.

· For **William Bittner** who without the chapter that he wrote, the book would not be complete. I appreciate how he shared his experience from his perspective in an open and honest way despite his career as a state policeman.

· In conclusion, I thank the editor, **Lois Ann Mast**, and her staff for accepting this manuscript and facing the task of publishing and distributing the book.

- The Author

— *Foreword* —

In the spring of 1985, my life and that of my family was turned upside down by a double tragedy that struck us suddenly and without warning. First, in late March, I was diagnosed with a potentially deadly form of cancer known as melanoma. Without any time to plan or prepare for what this illness might do to me, I was immediately scheduled for major surgery and went home just after Easter to recuperate. In all honesty, I was depressed and afraid. My relationship with God was an area that I had let slip over the years. Now with death staring me in the face, God became very important to me. As I struggled, little did I realize what I would soon need to face.

On the morning of April 17, 1985, as I lay in bed feeling very sorry for myself—home from the hospital just ten days—my two-year-old son Christopher was playing outside when all of a sudden I panicked when I heard some unearthly screams.The screaming was hysterical, and I know that something was terribly wrong. As much as I wanted to deny it, I also knew the screams were my wife's. I ran to my bedroom door and noticed that the front door was wide open—another signal that something was terribly wrong on that cold spring morning. Suddenly, my wife ran in through the door, grabbed the phone, and cried out, "Dear God, please send help! Christopher is dead!"

I ran outside and saw my son lying on his back in our driveway. A large truck was stopped along the road just beyond his body. The connection was obvious, although my mind fought to deny it. Christopher had been run over by the truck.

As I knelt beside Christopher, and looked into his death-stilled face, I realized that this was only his body now. His precious spirit was gone. And from that moment on, I personally began a long journey of recovery and sorting out my faith that continues to today.

As part of my healing process, that began about three months after the accident, I began writing down the thoughts that always seemed to fill my head. I wrote about how I felt in the first hours, days, and weeks, following Christopher's death. About how his death was affecting my family. Eventually, I realized that what I was writing might be of help to others, and so I began shaping it into a book. My story did eventually become a book, *When Good-Bye Is Forever: Learning To Live Again After the Loss of a Child.*

Now I find myself, almost nine years after my son's death, writing this foreword for another book—a book by someone who has become our dear friend in the past years. Please let me explain how.

In 1992, we received a letter from an Amish family near Lititz, Pennsylvania, who had also experienced the death of a son in an accident similar to Christopher's. They had read *When Good-Bye Is Forever.* In February 1993, we visited with them—David, Esther, Jacob, Samuel, Amos, and Emma Smucker—at their farm. In the months since, we have been corresponding by mail and have visited them at their home several times. They also made a trip to our home in Vermont to visit us.

David and Esther are not strangers to sudden, unexpected death. David, Jr.'s death in May 1992 was not their first loss. Ten years earlier they lost another child, Johnny, to crib death. Esther's Aunt Naomi was tragically murdered. Like me, Esther in particular, has found that writing her thoughts about David, Jr.'s death has helped to sort out this happening in her life. Writing about losses such as these often helps the person who is writing to absorb them into the present reality, and helps to express both the pain and *the hope* which come from these events.

Esther has done something I also did in my book. She has asked her husband, her children, and a state policeman to write about the experience from *their* perspectives. Whose words can comfort a child who has lost a brother or sister better than those of another child who has also lost a brother or sister? Or, a father's words for another father?

Some would question whether we should air our experiences so openly. That's a fair question. Where do we look for an example on which to base our decision? The Bible should be our source. In it we find that Jesus set the example for us when He wept at the death of his friend Lazarus. He did not put on a stern, solemn face, and shroud His grief in silence. He wept openly.

A second question is, should we write about these happenings, or should we let them go in silence? God in His written, living Word seems to provide the answer. He has given us the full account of the grief of those who loved Jesus and saw Him crucified, who buried Him and mourned for Him. Certainly, we do not put ourselves on a level with God, but His Word which is shared with us is a wonderful—actually our only—source of hope in the face of death.

In our humanness, I believe He would have us share our experiences as a form of comfort to others. In fact, I believe He calls us to do so. Once again, I turn to His Word: "Blessed be God, even the Father of our Lord Jesus Christ, the Father of mercies, and the God of all comfort; Who comforteth us in all our tribulation, that we may be able to comfort them which are in any trouble by the comfort wherewith we ourselves are comforted of God (II Corinthians 1:3-4). What better way to reach those with whom direct contact is impossible than through the written Word?

And so Esther and her family have chosen to spread God's comfort in many ways. They join their brothers and sisters in Christ in visiting with so many families who have lost loved ones, and on a very personal level, they have written this story to comfort those who are facing grief.

In the pages that follow, you will find the account of the Smuckers' loss and some of their personal thoughts. But most importantly, you will find hope that is only available in Jesus Christ our Lord and Savior. Join David, Esther, Jacob, Samuel, Amos, and State Trooper William Bittner now as they open their hearts and lives to you.

- John Bramblett
Author of *When Good-Bye Is Forever: Learning To Live Again After the Loss of a Child*

Chapter 1

Good Night, My Son

As I gazed at the still form of our son, his body prepared for burial, I felt an overwhelming feeling of sadness. He looked beautiful and perfectly at peace in a suit of new clothes, all dressed in white. The color of his clothes seemed to reflect his whole life—purity.

But this was the first time he was dressed in all new clothes. I felt guilty and remorseful. It did not seem fair. He had never had new clothes, but had always worn the ones handed down after his three brothers had outgrown them. Being his mother, I could only cry, "Now he gets new clothes. Oh, how I'd love to see his face beam as he puts them on!" I could find peace only as I tried to picture him, in that Beautiful Land called Heaven, attired in beauty, which "we" can only imagine.

Now we were once again a fragmented family. Ten years ago our son Johnnie also lay in a coffin, in this same room, dressed for burial. His was a brief, sweet life, as the passing of a beautiful bud. After three and one-half years of marriage, we had been blessed with identical twin sons, whom we named Jacob and John. They were five weeks premature and weighed a mere four pounds each at three days old when we brought them home from the hospital.

It was a struggle for survival for us and the babies for several weeks. We needed to waken them every two and one-half hours and give them one ounce of formula until they weighed five pounds. It was so hard to awaken them as they simply wanted to sleep. I remember particularly one morning when I said to my husband David in despair, "I'm afraid Johnnie will just sleep his life away." It was so exhausting to give them the required amount of milk. They lacked the strength to nurse as normal babies would.

David went to call the doctor and tell her my fears. She came out that day and gave me fresh courage. Little did I realize how true my statement would be seven months later.

1

Those first six months were the busy months of summer. But, in spite of all the extra work, we enjoyed the twins so much and they brought us much pleasure. They really changed that first half year—from tiny, helpless infants to crawling, happy little boys. During those seven months of their lives together they never slept through the night.

*   *   *

On the evening of November 18, 1981, we had taken the twins out to the cow stable, as usual. They observed everything. Johnnie had a way of looking at you that made you think he saw way beyond his young age.

That particular evening he was so sober. His ready, quick smile was just not there. His dad teased him by touching his cheeks and asking, "Where is your smile? Is your smile hidden somewhere in there?" He coaxed for a smile, but to no avail. Johnnie was just so very sober. That expression on his face is still very clear to me.

Early in the wee hours of the morning of November 19, 1981, I found Johnnie in his crib; his body was stiff in death. No words can describe the horrors of such a shock! It was dark and I reached in the crib to pick him up, thinking it strange that he had not awakened with his brother to be fed. When I picked him up, his arms and hands were stiff; he was drenched with sweat. I quickly laid him down and ran to tell David.

Something that takes only a minute or seconds to happen, like a death of a loved one, may take years to grasp or struggle with. After Johnnie's death, I struggled with fears that can not be explained to one who has never had a similar experience. Every time Jacob would cry, I'd hear Johnnie's echo in the back room.

We had to get rid of his crib. I believe those feelings of fear were the result of receiving such a severe shock in the dark. After endless nights of little sleep, my body was weakened. All that had taken its toll. A long, miserable winter lay ahead. It was only by the grace of God that we survived with our sanity and the emotional scars healed.

Johnnie died of crib death, known as SIDS (Sudden Infant Death Syndrome). There is still much research being done to find the cause of this mysterious type of death that claims the lives of thousands of babies each year. So far, people doing research on SIDS have not come up

2

with any logical answers; they have only different theories. These twins, who had never been separated for even a day, were now separated forever in this life. Their lives had been entwined, woven together from the very beginning. They had also never been separated from me for even a day, being fully dependent upon me, who understood their needs and the sound of each of their cries. Now, suddenly our lives were broken apart and shattered. How could we ever get used to this sudden change?

Even now, every time I see a set of twins, I get that same ache in my heart, that of "remembering" and a deep longing to see my own together again.

After the sudden passing of our son, I felt sure my world would soon come to an end. Life had lost its meaning for us. However, life did go on, so we were also forced to go on with it. We had no way of knowing that we'd need to travel that same rough road again.

Over the following ten years, five children were added to our family. Our missing son was gone, but not forgotten. None of our other children came to "replace" him. Each was simply "another," with a personality of his own.

The day David and I were married, I remember being reminded it takes both sunny and rainy days to make a life complete. We have learned how true this is, in our spiritual lives as well as in material things. And we know not what the morrow brings. No, not even the next hours. To see one of your children go to his grave is one of the saddest, yet sweetest experiences one could have. It is sad because you miss him so much. You weep because of loneliness. It is sweet because you realize he must be very happy where he now is. However hard it is to bear, the feeling remains, "It is better to have loved and lost, than not to have loved at all."

— *Chapter 2* —

Little Angels

On April 23, 1987, a blond-haired, blue-eyed, pudgy-faced little boy was born and added to our family of sons. Now we had four sons and I remember thinking, "Now that makes two teams." I also remember thinking, "This just might be our last son." We named him after our great uncle, David E. Huyard, who was very special to us. The doctor asked us what the middle initial "E" stands for. So, I called my uncle and asked what his initial "E" represents. He laughed and said, "There is a story behind that." When he was born his parents said, "This is Enough!" and they named him David E. He was the youngest in the family. So it was family joke to us.

David, Jr., always seemed to bubble with joy with his contagious smile, so I started calling him "Bubbles." The name stuck and the boys and Dad named him "Bubbs." He was known to many only as Bubbles, until a few years ago when we called him Junior. From babyhood, he blended right into our family of boys.

By the time he was only a few years old, he was right there when they played baseball. It was especially cute to watch him when it was his turn to bat. He'd practice by swinging his bat, and then he'd "knock the plate" just like a pro. When he hit the ball, he'd run for first base, his white hair flying, coat hanging open, and his shoestrings flapping loose. Typical boy-fashion!

When he was three and one-half years old, our first and only daughter was born. We named her Emma. Junior and Emma became close playmates and were good company for each other. He loved her and cared for her tenderly.

Where we live, the road separates the house and barn. There is much traffic and much speed. It has always concerned us to live like this, even though we got used to it, to a certain extent. My mind was never at ease when the children were outdoors. We taught them all at an early age what the road is and how to cross it carefully. We can be as careful as we wish, but it is still dangerous to live in a situation like this.

When Emma was old enough to walk and also go to the barn, Junior was simply her guardian and kept her off the road. It was a common sight to see them, hand in hand, out in the barn or swinging on the swings. They did this when the other boys were in school.

I'd often think what a beautiful, precious time in childhood it is at the age of four and five years. Children are capable of doing so much, learning responsibilities, while at the same time they are still funny without being arrogant or conceited. They are not yet exposed to the peer pressure that is often so prevalent when they start school. Junior would sit for hours on a chair watching me sew, and we'd chat, or he would sing. After I'd finish sewing some garments, I'd ask him, "Now will you please turn these inside out?" In return, his eyes would twinkle and he'd say, "You mean outside in!" It was a game we shared.

I learned to know Junior personally during the school months. He was a very careful little boy and one who thought deeply. He developed a personality all his own and was truly exceptional for one so young. He was very patient and had unusually deep blue, trusting eyes. I learned so much from him.

In October of 1990 I wrote an entry in my diary that Junior suddenly said to me, "I want to go to Heaven." I asked him what he wanted to do there. He said he wanted to play with Jesus. (He was only three years old.)

In December of that same year Junior asked me, "Mom, when little children die, they become angels, not?"

I said, "Oh, yes!"

Then six-year-old Samuel added, "Yes, they go to Heaven because they did not sin. They are too little."

I now wonder if his thoughts were often on that subject as he sat on his rocker, thinking and rocking away.

Three years later, on a warm, sunny day, Junior and I were in the garden. The date was May 21, 1992, and it was Thursday. I was hoeing weeds in the garden, and Junior was trailing beside me, hands in his pockets. We were exchanging bits of conversation as I worked. I was fully aware of his presence, and it would have seemed empty without him near.

I used to call him "my little puppy," and he'd grin back. As I worked, my thoughts were not on deep things. Apparently his must have been, for he suddenly told me he was going to Heaven. I replied, "You'll go some day."

5

He said he wanted to go now, and wondered what he must do to get there. I said, "Believe on Jesus and love everybody."

He replied, "Oh, I do! And everybody loves me." Then he added that some little girls like little boys, too.

I asked him what he had in mind. He answered, "My two cousins, Rebecca and Mary love me."

It amused me and I told him he was funny. Then he wondered, "How will I go to Heaven?"

I answered, "With your wings."

He thought a bit, then said, "When daddys die, they are big angels; when little boys die, they are little angels."

I asked, "You mean like your brother Johnny who is an angel in Heaven?"

It occurred to me that we had never really told him he had a brother who died, so I thought, "Here is my chance to tell him about John." I figured he was old enough to understand.

But it took no explaining as he told me very precisely that John is so big an angel. I was hoeing and had not looked up from my work. He earnestly said, "Look, Mom! He's so big an angel." He demonstrated with his hands; he held them about level with his chest.

As I looked at him and into his big, clear blue eyes, I got the feeling that he knew something that I didn't know. I asked, "How do you know that?"

He answered, "I just do."

I suddenly felt an inspiration from God and felt His nearness, feeling "this means something."

I leaned on my hoe and gave him my full attention. I thought back to my younger years when I used to think of death as a "monster" and was very afraid of it. I did not want my children to grow up and be at death's door and fear death. So I said, "All right, Junior boy, if ever an angel comes for you—**don't be afraid**; just take his hand and go with him."

That fully satisfied him.

I kept this all in my heart and felt that Junior would leave us soon. At that time, I felt he would get sick. That evening I wrote down our conversation, since I thought it was so unusual.

The next day at the dinner table he brought up the subject about angels again when the family was all together. Junior wondered if there are houses in Heaven. I said, "I believe there are many beautiful mansions there and streets of gold."

Then he wondered about trees or flowers.

"Yes, I believe there are lots of pretty flowers and fruit trees there," I told him. One of the boys wondered if we will eat up there. Then Junior said with a grin, "Wouldn't that look funny, everyone sitting around the table with wings! What would we do with our wings?" We all laughed and Dad said, "I believe that would be taken care of." Later this conversation proved to be much consolation to us and to each of the boys.

The school term expired that same week and the school picnic was held the nineteenth at Amos Ebersol's. It was a perfectly lovely day. The men played baseball, challenging the upper grade boys in school. The women watched and visited. We all had fun!

Later, David said the best memory he has was on the day of the picnic when Junior was riding a small scooter. A steep slope going toward the house was perfect for little boys to coast down, and Junior made the best of it. David said that for some reason he just stood there and watched him for quite a while. Junior would walk up the hill with the scooter and then coast down, his white hair flying, and having the time of his life.

In looking back through my daily diary, I had made an entry for that day: "A good school term ended for the boys, but I am so glad to have our family together at home." Little did I realize then how quickly that would all change.

It seemed the parents were all reluctant to part the day of the picnic. We all had such a happy time together. Before we left, one of the mothers said to me, "Now when do we see each other again?"

My answer was, "I don't know, but don't wait so long to come."

Since that time, I am very limited with my "good-byes."

Two days after the school picnic, one of the school parents, a neighbor, was kicked in the face by a mule. He was in a coma for days and had a struggle for survival. We went over one afternoon to see if we could be of help. Other neighbors were there, baling hay. On Saturday of that week, David and the three oldest boys went to help bale hay in the afternoon. Junior, Emma, and I went to one of our other neighbors with some things. We walked with the express wagon in tow. It was a very nice day for a walk and I kept thinking, "Why don't we do this more often?" It felt good to the mind, body, and soul to enjoy the fresh air and sunshine.

We chatted along the way, and Junior pulled back on the wagon to brake it while going downhill. From a distance we saw Dad and the boys coming home with the big wagon. I asked Junior if he wanted to run down to meet them and ride with them. As was so characteristic of him, he thought a bit, then said, "No, I'll stay and go with you."

The memory of that enjoyable walk stays with me—just as do each hour and even the minutes of the following days.

This was the beginning of a series of accidents that occurred in the neighborhood, all within a radius of about two miles. One person was seriously hurt and three people were killed all in a period of less than a month. Two were five-year-old boys and the last one was a seventy-six-year-old Mennonite lady. She and her husband came to shake our hands and view our little boy after his death; three weeks later we went to her own viewing.

The specter of death seemed to hover ominously over the neighborhood. I believe that many hearts were in awe; perhaps, some in fear, and many with questions. But, who could we question? Was it the power of the Almighty? Or was it the Adversary? Our faith was surely put to test. It was an experience that I believe the entire neighborhood will never forget. It is my feeling that it created a bond such as we had never known before.

How fortunate we are to live in a neighborhood where people have caring hearts. Without these experiences, we would probably never have fully come to this knowledge.

— Chapter 3 —

Premonition

On Sunday, May 24th, we all attended church services in our district. We went in the open spring wagon, as our carriage was at a carriage shop to be repainted. It was cool so we took thick blankets along for the boys in the back.

That day we had visiting ministers. I happened to be sitting right next to where the minister stood to preach. After the services were over, Junior walked right over to me, and later different people said they have such a good memory of him as he walked past them to come to me while the people were still seated.

The minister's sermon that day was very timely, and I have no doubt in my mind that it was a direct leading from God that he was sent to our church that day. The Spirit of God must have directed his thoughts and words. His subject was on "death." This minister had buried a son who was killed in a farm accident some years ago. We had visited with them numerous times; we had things in common, as we had both lost a son. He talked of death as a "release" from this world, as a friend and not an enemy. He quoted, "Death is the door to Life." We need not be afraid if we are prepared to die. In a written prayer it says, "We should await His Glorious Coming with joy…."

I drank in every word. He told of how he was at the funeral of a girl in a western state. The minister had said that day, "If this girl believed in Jesus and was prepared to die, then death was the biggest and best gift that God could give her."

It brought tears to my eyes, and I thought of our son Johnnie who had left us so suddenly ten years ago. Now, here was a great consolation, and it filled my soul with peace. Nothing gloomy to think over—only peace and joy in the face of death. My heart felt thankful, even with the rather uneasy feelings I received after my conversation with Junior the week before. Now I felt I could accept his death. For those premonitions of his impending parting never left me, and I felt it could only mean his death.

Before we left church for home, I really wished for the chance to tell this minister how effective these words were and what it meant to me. I had no chance, so I told his wife to tell him that I agreed with his sermon on death, bringing out the hope and peaceful part of it. I told her I don't want any of my children to ever come to death's door and panic. Then I told her of my conversation with Junior the week before. Otherwise, I had told no one else but David. I felt the minister's wife would understand, since her thoughts had also often been of death and Heaven, and the mysteries of it.

It started to drizzle that afternoon, so we decided to go home before it rained more. Later we were told the boys at church had such a good picture of Junior when we hitched up to leave. Our four boys climbed into the back of the open wagon in full view of their friends, and Junior stood there and really waved good-bye to all.

By the next evening Junior had left this earthly land and joined the angels in that land of beautiful flowers and mansions, where there is no darkness. Jesus Himself is the Light! A place where anyone who has loved ones there could ponder on for hours and hours. What a wonderful place it must be!

We can read: "The most that we can see here on this earth is the least that he hath made...." At Junior's viewing, the visiting minister and his wife came, and words were inadequate as they held our hands in sympathy. The first thing she asked was, "Was this the little boy you told me about in church on Sunday?" I replied, "Oh, yes!"

To God be honor and glory for sending miracles in our day, in this dark world, where His Light is too often dimmed by our own earthly thoughts and goals. This particular happening left us in awe, and very thankful that He cared enough to send such a happening, so we might recognize His presence. It helped to strengthen our faith, erasing those feelings of doubts that at time invaded our thoughts. Was this part of God's purpose revealed to us? It has been a great consolation to us. We were inclined to cling fast to any threads of light that could bring comfort to our grief-filled hearts.

This happening, and many others following Junior's death, only proved to us more the existence of God, and that things don't "just happen," but are planned and molded by His hand to fulfill His patterns. Anyone who has experienced premonitions of any kind and felt His presence in super-human ways **knows** it's not only a dream or illusion. It is real, and we recognize it as the voice of God.

To verify this, I probably need to explain one other incident in particular. I don't know why this happened to me, as I had no such feelings on my mind at the time. I only know it was not a dream or illusion.

Two months before Junior's death, I heard beautiful singing in the distance. I looked in different rooms and upstairs. I called Junior by name since I thought maybe he was in another room singing, even though I knew he was in the barn with his dad. This happened three times, and each time I got up and opened doors. I also opened the kitchen door and looked outdoors. But no one was around. It puzzled me and gave me a bit of a scary feeling. I told no one, but felt this had a meaning. I pondered over its meaning as the days went by. I now think that God knew I needed to be prepared, in a sense, for the change that would take place in our lives.

Again, I cannot explain why this happened, but it has been a great comfort to me. Although a mystery, I am willing to let it go at that. But to be realistic, are such happenings any harder to explain or understand than the split-second timing of a death—when only one second later or sooner would have meant the difference between life or death? One "wills" it to have been a second later or sooner, but no amount of human reasoning or thinking will alter a loved one's death; so, again and again, one tries to shut the mind and continue on for the present.

And when you have come to the end of trying to figure out some supernatural event, you realize it is not a natural "happening of chance." It leaves you totally in awe of the One above. You sense the significance of the meaning. These are all reminders of a loving God, and you can almost feel His comforting hand as you sense His nearness.

As we face death and accept it as the ultimate victory of life, we can attain a certain amount of peace. It is the only way we can continue to grow spiritually. We have one of several choices to make. Either we can gain from painful experiences, or we can become bitter and question the existence of an Almighty God. By choosing the latter, we will have more questions than answers.

The experience of partings in death is universal. We all know it affects "individuals, no matter in what society they live. A bond can be created among individuals who suffer similar experiences, no matter who they are. This was proven to us many times by the many different people we met. The separation of loved ones, nevertheless, brings a

11

pain so sharp that it seems to cut the heart. Thinking of the victory and joys your loved one now has makes it easier. But, we are still here as humans and need to go through this, physically and emotionally. It is a traumatic experience and many times depletes your strength. However, all this is possible.

A verse in Romans 8 comes to my mind. By faith we can be reassured that..."All things work together for good for them that love God." ALL things! Can we pretend to understand that statement? We need to think of that verse on "down" days and moments. To continue with the verse "all things working together," it does not mean one particular happening in your life; but, it could mean a series of unfolding events all through our lives. And we need to trust Him who is in control.

We all know the feelings of pain, each in various circumstances. Feelings of pain and sadness help us to be understanding of anyone who suffers. We are aware of this caring feeling, a sharing of hearts, only if we share our pain, whatever it may be, rather than trying to avoid others or suffer alone. And if we share it, our burdens are lightened. If we try to carry these burdens alone, they are so heavy. By sharing them, they become lighter.

Chapter 4

My Life and Love Was Full

As we drove home from church that Sunday, our hearts felt lighter than they have since. The boys covered themselves with blankets and peeped out. They pretended they were riding in a Conestoga wagon and the weather was bad. They had a grand time. In fact, so much so that we had to remind them to quiet down for fear of passersby wondering what we were hauling in the back of our wagon! I can still hear Junior's voice, so clear, right with the noise of the others.

After we were home and in the house, the boys had more fun. I asked them if they brought my wagon in (I meant my bag), whereupon they all laughed, and Junior wrinkled up his nose and giggled at me.

Later that day the boys were all outdoors except Junior, who was sitting on his small rocker and singing. I was by the sink and stopped what I was doing and just listened, thinking, "How does he know all the words to that song?" He was singing "Jesus Loves Me," without faltering, all the way through. His voice was clear and musical, and I hope that memory will always stay with me.

He loved to sing already at three years old, and was able to keep a tune. Singing was just a part of him. He had two favorites. Before he could pronounce the words properly, he used to sing:

> *O what wondrous Love I see*
> *Freely shown for you and me,*
> *By the One who did atone.*
> *Prostrate on His sacred face,*
> *Jesus suffered for the race,*
> *In Gethsemane, alone.*

> Chorus:
> *O what Love, Matchless Love,*
> *O what Love, for me was shown;*
> *His forever I will be,*
> *For the Love He gave to me,*
> *When He suffered, all alone.*

He also sang:

> *Angels rock me to sleep*
> *In the cradle of Love,*
> *Bear me over the deep*
> *To that haven above.*
> *When the shadows shall fall*
> *And the Saviour shall call,*
> *Angels rock me to sleep*
> *In the cradle of Love.*

But the song he loved the most was: "Just A Little While To Stay Here...."

Ever since the boys slept upstairs, their dad would take them up, tuck them in their beds, and help them with their prayers. They all slept in one room. Jacob and Junior slept in one bed, and Samuel and Amos shared the other bed. They always wanted their dad to sing a few songs before he came down. That singing drifted down to me and was many times an antidote of calmness for me after a busy or hectic day. Before he came down he'd say, "Good night," and usually only Samuel would answer. The other boys were already asleep.

Recently, I asked David what song Junior used to pick. He said Junior always begged him to sing, "Just a Little While to Stay Here." Very fitting words as I think upon them now:

> *Soon this Life will all be over;*
> *And our pilgrimage will end.*
> *Soon we'll take our Heavenly journey,*
> *Be at Home again with friends;*
> *Heaven's gates are standing open,*
> *Waiting for our entrance there.*
> *Some sweet day we're going over,*
> *All the beauties there to share....*

Now that song is for us.

As I consider the changes and adjustments Junior's death brought to our normal lives, one scene is especially painful to me and always makes me lonesome for him.

Our children are all lovers of stories and books. Ever since they were old enough to comprehend, they'd beg for bedtime stories. I probably enjoyed it as much as they did. The boys would pack against me on either side on the sofa, and Junior would plop on my lap, his white, tussled hair in my face with strands of hair twitching my lips

14

at times. Little one-year-old Emma sometimes would come meddling, vying for full attention, trying to push Junior off. He usually said nothing, but stayed sitting placidly on my lap. And my life and love was full....

Now I miss that warm little body, leaning against me at the close of the day, and storytime has lost some of its flavor for me.

The boys wanted me to read in Amish (meaning Pennsylvania Dutch), since Junior could not yet understand English. So, I would interpret in Dutch as I read in English. Now, with seven- and eight-year-old Samuel and Amos, I only read in English. I anticipate the time two-year-old Emma will say, "Read in Amish!"

— Chapter 5 —

"I'm Going To Heaven, Mom"

Monday morning, May 24, 1992, was Memorial Day. It was a very chilly morning, and a light rain was falling. Each Memorial Day Weaver's Dry Goods Store has an annual yard sale, which usually draws a crowd. I decided to go that morning. It was early when I went to the boys' room and silently shook Jacob awake. I asked him if he wanted to go with me. I did not want to take all the boys along, yet I wanted a helper if I took the horse and buggy. So, we left as soon as it was daylight.

There wasn't a big crowd there since it was drizzling and chilly. We looked around a bit and I bought a few pairs of shoes; I also bought a few other items. At one place there was a nice scooter for sale, like new. It caught Jacob's eye, and he begged for it. We passed by that stand, reluctantly. We toured the area, checking for items of interest. That scooter didn't leave my mind. Later we returned to that stand and looked at it again. Jacob told me they have only one scooter to share with four boys, and this one was just like the one they had at home.

For a minute I was tempted to wish I hadn't brought him along. But, I realized that what he said was true; it **would** be nice to have another one to play with, when I looked at it through the eyes of a little boy. So I relented and bought the scooter.

Another "guidance" of God's hands…. I was quite oblivious to what a major role that scooter would have in bringing about such a drastic change to our lives.

As soon as we arrived home, the boys surrounded me and wanted to see everything. I had bought a pair of shoes for Junior that I thought he could wear the next winter. He tried them on right away and stepped proudly around in them saying, "Oh, thank you, Mom!"

They were all excited about the new scooter and soon were headed for the barn, and I saw little of them for the rest of the day. It was so nice to have all the boys at home. Our summer on the farm had begun.

16

After our return from the yard sale, the sun appeared from behind the clouds. I did the laundry and baked several cakes; then I did something I never do on Mondays. I did most of the trimming around the yard that afternoon. The boys were mostly in the barn taking scooter rides. They said they were taking turns, two boys for ten minutes at a time. The game was on! At times they came over to the yard to me. David was planting corn that afternoon and asked if I'd do the milking while he kept on planting. The boys did their chores while I was milking the cows. Soon the boys were scooting around the cow stable and having a happy time, chasing each other as boys will do.

Several days before that, when I was doing the milking, Junior had helped me milk. Now as he went by I asked him, "Junior, aren't you going to help me milk the cows tonight?" He answered, "No, not tonight!" and away he went.

For awhile none of the boys were around. Then, suddenly Jacob came over to the sputnik (a stainless steel cart on wheels, where we pour the milk in from the milkers). He had a note and hid it on the sputnik, saying, "Don't tell the boys where the note is. We're having a treasure hunt." I asked what the treasure was, and he replied with a grin, "It's the new scooter." Then he left the cow stable.

After a while the three youngest boys came running for the sputnik, and soon found the note. They read it hurriedly and ran out the door, with Junior a few steps behind. I wished I could join in the hunt!

A little while later, Junior came in the cow stable to me and said he was cold. I said, "Well, button your coat." I helped him button up. Then he gave me a big hug and said, "I love you, Mom!" I hugged him back and said, "I love you, too!" With that he left the cow stable and I resumed the milking, feeling light of heart, thinking of his dear personality. I had no way of knowing that would be the last hug, the last words, the last time I'd see this dear one alive and warm. Those words, "I love you, Mom," were the last words he spoke to me. What a beautiful memory of him!

I had taken all the milkers off the cows except one. It was on the last cow. I was almost done. The time was 6:30. Suddenly my peace was shattered by terrible screams of fright from the boys! There was an urgency in their cries such as I had never heard before from anyone, and hope never to hear again.

I knew something awful had happened! They came running in through the doors at the far end of the cow stable, and all were trying to say something at the same time. They were crying hysterically. I cannot describe the frightened looks on their faces, or how my heart and mind were jolted, or the thoughts of what may have happened that raced through my mind! It was only a matter of seconds, yet I felt numb with shock. At that time I did not realize that Junior wasn't with them. Something seemed to have clogged in my throat and threatened to choke me. If you ever received an awful fright in an instant, you will know the feeling that engulfed me now. To this day I can't stand to hear any of the boys give a loud scream or yell.

I asked, "What happened?"

All their words were incoherent to me as they tried to talk while crying.

Again I spoke, this time to Jacob, the oldest. "Please calm down and tell me what's wrong."

He cried, "Junior was hit by a car!"

I asked nothing more and was too stunned to move. I could only picture him struggling. I've wondered since why I didn't ask if he was moving or how he looked. We can rehearse in our minds what we'd do or say in a case like this; but, no parents are trained to prepare for such a time. One cannot prepare himself for such a shock.

Before I made any move, a young man came running into the front door. He was crying and yelling, "Somebody call an ambulance!"

The next thing I remember saying was, "Go tell your dad," and I immediately went to the phone and dialed 911. I was only a few feet away from the phone, which is in the cow stable. So very little time elapsed until they received the call. In my dazed mind, I'm not sure what I did next. Only I felt I could not go out to the road. I felt I simply couldn't stand to see him struggling or badly mangled.

Finally, I thought I would still want to say bye-bye to him. I slowly went out the milkhouse door and around the silo. There I stopped, for he was in plain view across the road, lying in the gutter on his back. Even from there I could see he wasn't moving.

Slowly I crossed the road and went over to him. I only stroked his one hand and gazed down at him. He looked almost peaceful, with both arms thrown back and his legs crossed as if he were asleep.

The only real sign of injury was the blood gurgling out of his mouth. His eyes were partially open and as I looked into them, I realized he was gone. Instantly, his words came back to me, "I'm going to Heaven, Mom," and I just knew his dreams were fulfilled.

I was filled with a calm I cannot describe. I felt a presence around me that controlled me. Rather, it was a feeling of awe, that this is sacred. The presence of God was so strongly felt. The best way I can explain that controlled feeling is, when your own strength fails, you draw from an inner strength that is not your own. It is divine help.

I can give no other logical reason why I didn't simply scream! I also remember thinking, "I don't want him to hear his mother screaming when an angel comes for him." This was very clear to me, and I didn't utter a sound. I also knew you don't move accident victims. Meanwhile, the young driver of the car was running up and down the road, crying. He was yelling, "Now I'm in trouble. Now I'll go to jail." Then he yelled at me, "It's no use, can't you see he's dead!"

Cold, stark words. Yet, I still felt no fear, only calmness. I glanced over at Junior and said to the driver, "I think I saw him move his hand," simply to console him. I've often wondered if it actually moved, or if it was only a reflex. I realized the young man needed comfort right then.

What happened next is something I've often pondered over since, as I knew it wasn't myself, but someone within me that prompted me to go over to this young man. I hugged him as I told him, "I'll tell you a secret." Then I told him how Junior had told me he's going to Heaven. I added, "And now he's there! You were just a tool." I wasn't sure if he really heard me, but he calmed down somewhat. I felt no malice toward him, only love, and I promised him he would **not** go to jail.

What happened next isn't very clear to me now. I remember traffic going by, and it bothered me a lot. I felt that if Junior had been lying in the middle of the road they would have driven right over him. I looked up the road, wondering why the ambulance didn't arrive. Then I went back to the phone and again dialed 911 and asked if the ambulance wasn't coming. The lady assured me it was on the way. It was then I realized I still had one milker on a cow. I quickly went and took off the milker and set it in the aisle.

Meanwhile, little twenty-month-old Emma was hanging onto my skirts and crying. She seemed to sense that something was wrong. I've often wondered what went through her little mind as she saw Junior lying there. I picked her up and carried her with me wherever I went, but she kept on crying.

I again went back to where Junior lay. Now it seemed I couldn't leave him. It was that natural instinct to try and protect him. In the distance I heard sirens. I remember a stranger asking me if my husband was around. I told him he was in the field. He ran for the field.

Meanwhile, David was out at the far end of the field, oblivious to all the activity until he saw Jacob, Samuel, and Amos running toward him in the distance. They were all crying and stumbling as they ran. But they picked themselves up and continued to run, their tear-streaked faces dirty. When they reached him, one of them cried, "Junior has been hit!" Another cried, "Junior's dead!" Another cried, "His tongue is cut in half."

David said his first thoughts were denial. "Oh, it's not that serious," or "It can't be that bad." Then he had a feeling of panic. Suddenly, he had a completely warm feeling that enveloped his whole being. Something told him, "Everything's taken care of. He's going to be all right." He thought then that Junior would be taken to the hospital and would soon be all right. But later, David realized that the feeling meant, "He **was** taken care of and at peace."

David's first impulse was to leave the team and run, but then this warm feeling came over him and calmed his panic. The horses walked all the way in, and the boys again ran back in before him. He handed the reins to Jacob and told him to tie them by the barn; then he came running to join me where Junior lay.

We exchanged no words, but he went down on his knees and knelt by his little son and took his hand. So very gently he took Junior's small hand in both of his and said softly, "Junior, this is Daddy. Can you hear me?"

There was simply no response as Junior's once beautiful eyes looked far away into the distance. I kept thinking, "Can't he see the child is gone!" But, I still said nothing.

Just then a man ran up to us and said he was from the fire company. He looked into the pupils of Junior's eyes, and I could see he felt the situation was desperate. He told David to keep talking to him. He said he found a pulse and kept looking up the road, saying Junior desperately needed suction. I remember another young man standing by whose legs were shaking. The fireman started to administer artificial resuscitation. He blew only once into Junior's mouth.

At that time it seemed some sense of peace left me as I realized they would try to revive him, when I felt sure he had gone to that

Beautiful Land. I only wished with all my heart that he could go in peace. I told this stranger, "If he is gone, please let him go."

Yet, I also realized that from a medical viewpoint they needed to work for survival until all else failed. I'm thankful I did not need to see what followed in the next few hours—the standard procedures to try and revive critically injured people. However, I still highly respect the ambulance and fire personnel as I realize many lives are saved and helped because of their unselfish efforts. The next time I looked up I saw a few of our neighbor men walking toward us. As I looked around, I suddenly noticed vehicles parked around, but I never remembered seeing any pull up or stop.

A policeman came over to me just as the ambulance arrived. Several medical personnel came over and examined Junior. They cut his clothing off and gently put a collar around his neck. Their actions were swift but gentle. As they worked, the policeman asked me if I was his mother. Then he asked our names and address and the child's name and age. I could hardly concentrate and could not tell him the year he was born. I only said, "Well, he's five years old." I kept my eyes on Junior.

So, quickly they said, "Let's go," and in unison, four people put their hands under him and laid him on a stretcher. I whispered, "Bye-bye, Junior," as he was loaded into the ambulance.

There was a hurried consultation as to who would go with what vehicle. David looked at me and asked if I wanted to go along.

I said, "No, you go."

I did not want to go along to the hospital, as I knew we couldn't both leave our crying children feeling abandoned. He got in the front seat with the driver, and they drove away. My gaze lingered as I watched them leave. I felt a deep sadness mingled with anxiety.

Chapter 6

Love In Action

I looked around, wondering where the boys were. They were standing on the barn hill, outside the big doors, and all were crying quietly.

I also wondered what happened to the young man who had hit Junior. I then noticed several police cars, and the feeling came to me, "All this activity." It seemed like an intrusion into our private lives. Later, I realized what an utterly false assumption this was, as the State Police proved to be dear friends to us in the months to come. They are caring human beings who feel, think, and hurt deeply, just like we do, but are trained and expected to maintain their dignity and composure in any situation they may chance to meet.

I suddenly realized I should make a few phone calls, so I went to the barn again and notified David's parents and my parents. I told them, "If only someone would come and stay with the children." I went out to the road again with the intention of finding the young man. Not in my wildest imagination could I imagine how he must be feeling; however, I knew it must be hard.

As I walked around his car, a state trooper was walking toward me. I shall never forget the look on his face. Later I could not remember any of these strangers' faces, but this face stood out in my memory. I felt he had the most compassionate look on his face I had ever seen! As we met, I told him to "please take care of the young man who was driving the car that struck our son." He promised he would and said, "I believe he did everything he could in order to be able to stop."

The trooper's name was William A. Bittner, and he was the investigating officer in this accident. We learned to respect and appreciate him, not only on duty, but as a dear friend later on. He showed wisdom, sensitivity, and a caring attitude for all involved.

As I started for the barn doors where the boys were, I noticed the young man, sitting in the back of a police car. I opened the door and again tried to comfort him. As I came to the boys, they were all crying. I gathered them all in my arms and said, "Let's go in the barn and pray together."

As they came crying to me, they must have felt I was their refuge and strength. I was reminded of how it must feel to our God in Heaven when we as adults seek His refuge and strength, and cry out to Him in deep distress or trouble.

When alone inside the barn, we all made a circle and dropped to our knees. Praying aloud, I pleaded to God for a submissive heart to accept whatever His will would be in the days ahead. I entrusted Junior completely into His care. Then I told the boys to be prepared that Junior might not come home again and live. I asked them if they thought they could be brave. With fresh tears, they nodded, and they did their best.

I then asked Jacob if he would go into the house for a bottle for Emma.

"Oh, no," he said, "I don't want to go into the house alone."

I should have known better.

The boys and I went down to the cow stable and I said, "Let's finish the chores."

As I walked about, I noticed neighbor after neighbor walking past me. No one said anything and neither did I. I did what was an outlet for my shock just at the moment. I kept busy. I started washing the milkers. Time had no meaning. I noticed a crowd of people out by the road, and wondered where they all came from. Later I learned one of the neighbors had a gathering along Hammercreek Road. They saw the blinking lights, and many came right over.

As I started washing the milkers, our neighbor Malinda came through the door and asked a few questions. She said she would wash the milkers. The neighbor men asked for instructions as to how to finish the chores. Others offered to give us rides to the hospital the next day. It is simply incredible what people did for us! I call it love in action. There is no way I can convey in words what this type of help meant to us. Many hands were there when we needed immediate help and our strength had failed. These people dropped their own work and plans and came to our aid.

As I went about my work, my mind refused to function, yet I felt perfectly in control. Things needed to be done and I knew it was up to me since David had left.

Just then my parents, David's parents, and my sister Rebecca walked in the door. As I saw the expressions on their faces my reserve broke, and I wept for the first time. The thought occurred to me, "This is actually happening; it is not only a dream." They asked how he was and I said, "It looked bad to me." Just then the phone rang. They looked at me, expecting me to answer it. Suddenly I felt afraid and I said, "One of you, go ahead."

Someone did and we all kept quiet. The caller was David. He said the nurse had just come to him and told him, "It doesn't look good." Then both my parents told me I should go to the hospital also. The thought had not occurred to me. I told them I felt I could do nothing for Junior; what would be the purpose? They said, "If you don't go for any other reason, then go for David's sake." I told them I can't leave the children. But they were adamant and said Rebecca would stay with them. They said they would go with me. So it was decided. They told me to go into the house and change clothes. By now it was dark and as we crossed the road, I was completely oblivious to any activity around me. I have no idea who came or went or if any vehicles were around yet, but I imagine there were.

When we came to the mailbox I saw Junior's one shoe and one stocking lying on the lane, close together. I stared in disbelief. How or when did they get there? They were a good distance away from where Junior had lain. It gave me a sickening feeling as I sensed this was the spot where our dear son had taken his last steps. Later, Trooper Bittner explained to us that that often happens in accidents. The force of the impact often causes people to lose their shoes or socks.

As I entered the house, I felt I had some cleaning up to do before I could leave, but my parents urged me to let things be and go.

I felt like a robot as I packed my bag with clean clothes for David. My parents' neighbor, Jean Tressler, who had brought them, said she would take us to the hospital. I remember I have often wondered how the children felt when I also left them; it tore at my heart. But I was so grateful to my sister and neighbor Malinda who stayed with them.

*   *   *

On the way to the hospital I had time to think. I then told them how Junior had said he wanted to go to Heaven. Otherwise, I can't remember any conversation. I started to shake and shook most of the way in.

When we arrived at the hospital I was at a loss as to where to go. Finally we found the emergency waiting room where the hospital chaplain opened the door to usher us in. Then I saw David, alone in the room. I searched his face for any sign of hope. He was very calm but grave. I kept thinking as the chaplain shut the door, "There is no hope or why would he be in there with David?"

David then said the doctor had just been in and told him, "Your son is brain dead, but he is on the breathing machine. They are taking more tests to prove nothing is functioning." I still did not fully realize the significance of that message. I kept thinking, "If he is dead, then why do they keep his heart going? Will he be a living vegetable?" My heart knew the meaning, but my mind refused to follow. I felt confused. I kept thinking, "I expected him to leave us sometime but not so soon and not in such a violent way!" My mother made several phone calls and so did David's mother. Again, time had no meaning. David's composure and calm voice helped us all as he was asked questions and made decisions.

After what seemed like a long time, Dr. Argires stepped into the room and his face was very serious. He told us our son was brain dead and it would be just a matter of removing the breathing machine until his heart stopped beating on its own.

David asked him what he'd do if it were his son. He said, "I'd remove the machine." He explained in roundabout ways what happens.

I realized later it was his way of preparing us for the word "death." Still I did not fully grasp the reality of it. I wanted to ask the vital question which lurked in back of my mind, "You mean Junior is dead?" But none of us asked and he did not say in plain words that our child had died. After he left, we were discussing what would we do next. David tried to tell us that Junior had died, but his mother asked, "Are you sure?" Later David told us that Dr. Argires had told him he believed Junior was killed instantly. My own feelings were then confirmed. Yet now, as we began to realize what the doctor meant, I could hardly wait until they took that respirator off him. It gave me a desperate feeling!

As we sat there, my twin sister and her husband came through the door, and she was weeping as she came to me. I comforted her as I said, "It's all right; he's in Heaven now."

Then I began to fully realize the truth. Our dear little boy was actually gone! Oh, dear little boy, have you actually left us? Did your dreams come true? And oh, what are you now doing?

A nurse came in and motioned to David and me and wondered if we'd like to see Junior again. She urged us to as I hesitated. As we walked out the door and down the hall, I saw a policeman sitting there and immediately recognized him as the one who had looked at me with such compassion. The same look was on his face now as we passed him. David and I both wept as we neared Junior. He was lying on a stretcher, submerged in tubes and machines. It was repulsive to me to see his chest move up and down, yet we knew he had died. His eyes had that same far away look; his color was ashen, and he was cold to the touch. I hated that feeling of coldness. We stroked his dear head, but I soon turned away, even as the scene etched itself in my mind forever.

It was the beginning of a series of feelings of "letting go" I knew would follow. Anyone who has come abruptly face to face with the death of his own flesh and blood knows the incredible feeling it creates. It's a searing pain that seems to cut right through the heart while you struggle to grasp all that happened. You, in reality, need to go on living. You keep thinking, "This simply can't be true, yet you know it is!" The sight of that still form is proof enough. Even that can't seem to penetrate the mind.

It takes many weeks and months to heal a broken heart. Years never erase the pain, even as it takes months to heal the wound of a severed arm or leg. But this wound is so invisible. How can anyone heal a wound that cannot be seen? Life is never the same again. Living on earth still has pleasant moments: its joys, its beauties, the rising and setting of the sun, the changing of the seasons. But something has been lost, and your perspective of life has changed forever. The old love for life will never fully return.

The rest of the family members were also allowed to see Junior. I don't know what their thoughts were.

Later my twin sister told me of the shock they encountered as they arrived at the hospital and searched the halls for us. They received the message of Junior's accident, but presumed he probably had broken bones. No thoughts of death crossed their minds. They thought they'd come in and see him and talk with him. When they asked the nurses where he was, they received evasive answers.

Finally a nurse said, "Here comes the doctor; ask him." So they asked the doctor, "How is the little boy?" He simply said, "I think you should be told—the child is dead." The shock must have been tremendous!

When we got back to the waiting room we started making some decisions. We decided I would go home while David stayed to sign the final papers. As we went out the door, a young man lying on a hospital bed in the emergency room, called me over to his bed. I wasn't prepared for his actions. His breath reeked of strong alcohol as he put his arms around me and pulled me down to him. All the time he kept saying, "I'm so sorry. I'm so sorry. I didn't know"

I told him, "It's alright. Our son is now in Heaven."

Then he wept and again said, "I'm so sorry." I had to pull myself away from him. One of the nurses stopped me in the hall and said, "The reason he is so upset is because he was making fun of you as he was wheeled past your door and saw you sitting there." His language was inappropriate and the nurses told him to stop as these people just lost a son to death. Now he wanted to apologize.

Who knows? Perhaps this was already an incident in touching someone's life through Junior's death. It was a scene I'll never forget. I wondered why this young man was brought to the hospital. As I glanced at the other beds, I saw suffering people. So much sadness and heartache. It made me want to hug and try to comfort them all. Inside the shelter and security of your own home it is hard to see the awful pain and suffering of many human lives. It is rather depressing to see so much pain in a hospital, yet at the same time it creates a longing and a deep love to help each suffering person. I had to think of how Jesus must have felt while on earth when the many maimed, crippled, blind, and sick came to Him to be healed. He must have felt the burden of the whole world on His shoulders. Don't we feel the same way at times, in a sense?

— Chapter 7 —

Teddy Bears In Time of Tragedy

At home, my sister tried to cheer up the boys. They tried to play a game of Memory; it didn't last long. They could not concentrate. Then she read stories to them, but neither could they concentrate on that. Soon Corporal Ramos from the Ephrata State Police Barracks arrived with a box of teddy bears. He let little Emma choose one for herself.

The boys later said that when the police arrived at the scene of the accident. a kind officer took them up to the barn hill and put his hand on their shoulders and told them to stay there. They were all questioned as to what they saw and heard. I can only imagine how frightened they must have been. Then the policemen took them to the trunks of their patrol cars and gave them each a teddy bear to keep. They asked if there were any more children. Jacob said they have one little sister, but she could have his teddy bear. What a beautiful gift for children who encounter tragedies.

Later Trooper Bittner explained to us that residents from a home for senior citizens wanted to do something for the community. Someone came up with the idea of making teddy bears for victims of traumatic experiences. The policemen each take a teddy in their patrol cars. The teddy bear represents security in traumatic situations for children. Children often form an immediate bond to them. It left me in awe at goodness in the hearts of people. Such an act of love! People reach out to fellow humans, total strangers.

Corporal Ramos kept the boys and my sister occupied for a while. His kindness will not be forgotten. It was special to us, and probably rewarding to him as well. The boys refused to go to bed. Finally, around 10:00, one of our neighbors and his wife came to the door and told my sister that Junior had died. They stayed at our house. When the boys were told, Amos, the youngest, immediately said, "Now he knows what the angels look like." Samuel's comment was, "Now he can't go to school." But Jacob, age eleven, reacted much like an adult. He really cried and said, "But we wanted him yet!"

As we prepared to leave the hospital, I hated to go home without David, but I also felt someone should go home since it was late. The nurses sent sedatives along home for the boys, hoping that they'd be able to get some sleep.

Just as we were leaving the hospital and were walking down the corridors, a doctor stopped us and asked if I knew how much Junior weighed. Hesitating only an instant, I replied, "Would fifty pounds sound right for a five-year-old?"

He said, "Yes, it does."

After he left I explained to the others, "This is strange, but just last week, out of the clear blue, Junior said to me, 'Mom, I weigh fifty pounds.'"

I didn't question him as to how he knew. We have no bathroom scales. Later I asked the boys if any of them took Junior out to the barn and weighed him on the platform scales. None of them had. Then how did he know? Call it ironic.

Chris Smith took us home. I must have gone into a state of shock en route because I shook uncontrollably all the way home. It felt good to sit between both mothers for warmth. Yet I was unable to voice my feelings and felt rather isolated in my thoughts.

It was 11:00 p.m. when we arrived home and there was very little activity there. It was hard for me to walk into the house as I tried to face the inevitable. Another one of our children had left us, never to come home again. Again I felt my throat constrict as a great lump formed. As I stepped inside the kitchen door, I thought at first that no one was around. But someone appeared from the adjoining room and I walked into the comforting presence of one of our ministers, who was also a neighbor. I just cried, and it already was a help to share grief. He also wept and said, "Think of the words in the sermon yesterday."

I said, "Yes, and it is true!" (Meaning, "There is no greater gift God could give than death to one of His own.") Here was another step in "letting go." There were a few more couples in the next room. Among them was a Horning Mennonite neighbor, who was also a minister, and his wife. Several of our brothers and sisters and a few more neighbors had also arrived by this time. Their presence meant a lot to me.

They introduced me to a non-Amish man who was a total stranger to me, also a minister. He said he was the father of the young man who was driving the car that struck Junior, and told me how sorry he was that this happened. I felt we shared a common bond, being parents of sons who were victims of circumstances that were completely out of our control. He talked about his son and said he felt his son was at a point in his life where he had decisions to make. He said his son was scheduled to leave for the Air Force in Texas the following Sunday, and he wished he would commit himself completely to the Lord before that time. He prayed a special prayer to God that something would happen to change his life. I kept thinking, "Is this another special message from God?—that of comfort in the presence of loss." I asked him, "Do you think this was your answer?" He admitted it probably was, and I noticed the sad look in his eyes, realizing that they and we would suffer because of it.

Who are we to protest against the divine will of God? We profess to believe and trust in Him. Here we could use some explanations. God is a **just** God. Even if it had not been His will to have a child hit by a car, He did permit it to happen. It would have been a very simple thing for Him to let that car be a second later, or to keep Junior moving instead of stopping.

Consider Job. Even if God did not plan all those afflictions in his life, He did allow them to happen. Satan did his best to try and destroy the strong faith that Job had in God. And God **did** strengthen Job through his trials because he trusted Him. Satan is mighty but God is Almighty! We need to bear this in mind whenever we become discouraged or confused. The story of Job has become very real to us. David has since bought a commentary on the book of Job because he loves the lessons it teaches.

It was getting late and someone suggested we make arrangements for the funeral and prepare papers to send word to relatives and friends. In the hospital we had already decided that the funeral would need to be on Wednesday because of Ascension Day being on Thursday. That meant there was only one day to prepare and one evening for the viewing. We had also decided who we wanted to officiate the funeral sermons.

We sat around the table and made notes of all the people we would notify of the death and funeral.

"Is this really happening or am I only dreaming?" At times it hit me full force!

I don't remember what time it was, but some time later we saw headlights turn into our driveway. As David walked through the door

I searched his face anxiously for signs of change. Was it actually still true, or had they removed the respirator and his heart kept beating? His calmness was a great strength to me even as I saw his expression revealing, "Yes, it is true."

He joined us at the table and we listed names until 1:30 a.m. My sister Rebecca and Emma and her husband planned to stay for the night. They were rocking the boys and little Emma, who still refused to go to bed. At 2:00 only Dan Kings and Crist Kings remained. As they got up and prepared to leave I was overwhelmed by a flashback. It was a scene from ten years ago. I cried, "You two people are the same people who first walked in the door after our Johnnie died. Now here you are again for the same reason, and I just can't believe it! That was ten years ago and now it seems like it has been only last week." We all wept together.

After they left, David took the boys to bed. They were very reluctant to go and we understood. We hoped they could at least rest if not sleep. Jacob now lay alone in his bed where the night before the warm body of his youngest brother had lain beside him. There would be no singing that night. It was a long time until their dad was able to sing to them again in bed.

So far our minds had been kept busy with necessities of how and when things should be done. It was actually a good time to make arrangements. In the stillness of the night there were no interruptions, and one could think clearly—as clearly as one is able to think under such circumstances.

When we finally went to bed we were emotionally exhausted. Now our thoughts went in scattered directions as we tried to comprehend what all had happened in so short a time. We began to wonder how it had happened and who had seen it happen. These were questions we hadn't asked the boys. We only put the logical reasons of the puzzle together over the following weeks and months. (By our own standards of human reasonings.)

We realized from past experience that we could not grasp what happened all in one night, or the enormity of the changes it would bring to our lives. Nor the acceptance of it—I cannot emphasize enough the importance of coming to terms with a sudden death bit by bit. Don't push yourself beyond your limits. Try not to become discouraged when life itself seems useless, even for over a year.

After our son Johnnie died, I became frustrated with myself for feelings I went through, yet kept them bottled within me. They were thoughts I never dared to share with others, fearing they would not understand. Finally, three months later, my doctor told me to not be so hard on myself. She told me, "To absorb such a shock, you need a whole year to heal from the shock alone, much less the grieving part." This was new to me and very helpful.

We need to allow ourselves enough time to recover. We are powerless to stop the pain and we learn it is useless to deny that it is there. Try not to think, "Now today I am going to accept this once and for all." You may find yourself in despair the next day. This is all very normal.

As you grieve, you go through stages of shock, disbelief, denial, anger, and hurt. Perhaps not in that order, but they will come. Shock and denial are often the first phases in a sudden death. Numbing seems to be the second phase. That sensation helps us through the funeral and the first following days. We can wear a mask on our face in the presence of others; nevertheless, these stages do take place and you need not give an excuse to anyone. Where there is love, there will also be understanding. Don't overreact to others' reactions concerning yourself. If anyone without experience tries to hint to you to be more accepting, try not to let it worry you. That can be very traumatic after you felt you **had** been trying. People mean well, and their intentions are good. We must realize they cannot feel our pain, even as we cannot feel pain or heartaches of others under other circumstances.

As we tried to rest that first night, our thoughts turned back in time to ten years ago, when we had tried to grasp such a shock the first night after Johnnie also left us so suddenly. "Oh God, why?" In a sense, it was even harder now since we realized what we still needed to face. Yet, in another sense, it was also helpful because we now understood grief better.

— *Chapter 8* —

Reflections At the Viewing

We did not sleep that night; we only tried to rest. We both got up around 5:00 the next morning. I felt nauseated and dizzy, and realized it was the result of shock.

There was a lot that needed to be done before people arrived, and I had not prepared our house for people. I knew a lot of activity would now take place. When David went out to the barn, several of the neighbors were already there, starting the chores. What a help! Neighbors and church people arrived early and expressed their sympathy. They carried out the furniture in preparation for the viewing and to accommodate the people. Many tears were shed and much was accomplished which we as parents could not have done alone.

We did not need to choose a burial site since we knew Junior would be buried beside his brother John's grave. Already I could envision two tombstones beside each other in that lonely graveyard.

Many people who came brought their children along. Already a longing was deep within me to see Junior again as my gaze followed these little children.

Soon after more of our family came, someone suggested making burial clothes. They needed his shirt, vest, and pants patterns. My mother-in-law had brought new white material. I suddenly realized that Junior would get a completely new set of clothing, and I had to cry, feeling a twinge of guilt. I cried, "He never got new clothes while he lived; now when he is gone he gets all new clothes!" It hurt me so much, as if I, his mother, had done him an injustice.

Just a few weeks before this I had made the four boys each a new summer shirt. It was the only new shirt I ever recall making for Junior, and he had worn it only one time. He had lots of shirts and pants, but they were all handed down after his brothers had outgrown them.

One of my sisters asked if Junior didn't like to wear used clothing. "Oh, no," I replied. "He never complained about it and never asked for new clothes or things. He was just content with whatever he got."

They tried to reassure me that it was only sensible to hand down clothing; however, it is a feeling of hurt that remains, and I would have loved to see his face beam at his new clothes. I believe he must be simply "radiant" in the transformed clothes he now wears as an angel. I especially liked the little white bowtie my sister-in-law made for him. He always looked like a small gentleman with the small black bowtie he wore for church. Now he was clothed all in white and had on a little white bowtie. I loved it! They made all his clothing so nice, and we really appreciated that they did this. I was perfectly content to let others do this for me.

Finally, around noontime we were told the undertaker was here with the body. My heart quickened as they placed his casket in the adjoining room. The undertaker motioned us to follow. He opened the casket and there lay Junior. But he was simply not there! He did look perfectly at peace. His fair young face had the same round cheeks and noble brow; his white hair looked so soft.

I inspected his face for everything familiar about him. There were his three scars, now clearly visible on his forehead from past minor accidents. I tenderly stroked his brow, and tears welled within me as I looked at his one scar. This particular scar held a precious story.

Only months earlier, he had fallen off a bench and hit his head on the sharp corner of our stove. The cut was so deep we felt it required stitches. At 9:00 in the evening David took him to the doctor's office. Later that evening they came home and Junior had his forehead bandaged and a smile on his face. David told me that Junior did not make a squeak or even a sound as the doctor injected a sharp needle right into his open wound several times to administer Novocaine. He said he told Junior to "hold tight to my hand and look at me." David said he held on very tight and looked trustingly into his daddy's eyes, and never made a sound; he only flinched a little.

Now here he lay, and all looked the same except it did not seem right to not see his beautiful big blue eyes. It appeared that he was merely asleep. Several months later our milk tester told us he had never viewed a corpse that looked like he was simply sleeping as our son did. We appreciated that he shared this thought with us.

The only visible signs of his fatal accident were a few marks on one cheek. Again I was thankful we could view him. We were told his death was due to a brain stem injury, but that he would have died from other internal injuries which were severe.

If felt good to have Junior here with us, even as he was. Perhaps, in our subconscious minds, we felt he was in our care again. I don't think the boys shared that feeling as they just looked and said nothing. Little Emma talked to him and tried to pry his eyes open—a similar game she had frequently played when Junior took a noon nap and she wanted him to wake up. Probably this was how she felt now. I've often wondered what went through her little mind.

Again, I tried to accept the enormity of the great change I knew would be inevitable in our daily lives.

The day went so fast as hundreds of people came to pay their last respects and share in sympathy. I have no idea when darkness fell, but suddenly I realized it was dark outdoors and I had no idea of the time. The boys were so tired, but refused to take naps. Samuel also refused to go in and see Junior again, and we did not force him.

People came from all walks of life to view Junior. Anyone from neighbors to feedmen, truckers to milkmen, or anyone who had any contact with us, and all were appreciated. Many came who shared similar experiences and needed only to hold our hands. It was especially touching when school parents and their children came. We held Samuel and Amos on our laps most of the time, and Jacob sat nearby. Probably the brightest spot of the day for the boys was when their school pals walked by. After one of the parents walked by with their two sons, Samuel whispered to his dad, "Daddy, Duane smiled at me." We suddenly realized that was probably one of the only times that day that anyone had smiled at them. All they had seen were sad faces. That really brightened him up for the moment. We asked if they would like to go and play with their school pals, and they wanted to.

It was 10:00 that night when the last people left. We were exhausted and had headaches. I felt rather gloomy and somewhere in the back of my mind lurked the thought. "It happened once, it happened twice, how can we be sure it won't happen again?" In my tired state of mind I felt it would be impossible to handle that!

I finally decided that time would be a factor in helping us cope with such gloomy thoughts as well as other thoughts. Only then did I find peace amid the storm. I felt very sad after the people left. Maybe they had been a physical prop for us; being able to share had been helpful.

We both slept some that night but were up early the next morning.

Chapter 9

Our Loss Was His Gain

The date was May 27, 1992. This was the morning of our dear son David, Jr.'s funeral.

Before people arrived, David and I gathered the children around us and explained to them what all would happen that day. We wanted to prepare them for the burial of their brother in a way that they could somehow realize the peace behind it and not the horror. We explained how his body would be buried in the ground, but that it was only the body which Junior lived in on "this" earth. He now has a new body in Heaven. They seemed to understand, or perhaps tried to convince themselves even as we tried to convince ourselves of this reality. Amos, the youngest one, said, "That is only the 'outside' of him; the inside of him went to Heaven." That was a simple version and we were glad he said it.

We were hoping that the young man who struck him would come sometime. That morning his parents came to view Junior. I was glad they came as I felt it would promote healing; however, their son did not want to come; he said he had seen enough.

After they left, my sister-in-law gave me an envelope, weeping as she handed it to me. I asked where she got it and she said a man had stopped by the driveway and gave it to her husband. I opened the envelope and found a sympathy card signed, "Justin." Now I understood and also wept.

I will need to explain why this card touched me so much. On the previous March 25th we had gone to Hershey Medical Center to visit our seven-year-old nephew (a son of the sister-in-law who gave me the envelope) who was there for observation. His parents had told us their neighbor, a total stranger to us, would pick us up. I had baked Boston cream pies that morning and set one on the table to eat when this stranger came to the door. We invited him in and he introduced himself. I offered him a piece of pie, which he readily accepted and for which he had complimented me greatly.

We left for Hershey, taking only David, Jr., with us to visit his cousin. He sat quietly on the back seat with me. We learned to know this man quickly and were really amused at him. He told stories of how he used to be an airplane pilot and did all kinds of stunts. He insisted he wanted to take us for a plane ride someday, but I told him I was fearful of heights. With that he insisted even more that I should give it a try. We joked about that for awhile.

We had a nice visit at the hospital and Junior and his cousin played games together. They played Memory, which was Junior's favorite. I had to wonder about the future of this little nephew who had seen many days as a patient in the hospital.

On the way home we again conversed about airplanes, and I told him that we had read in the morning paper at the hospital of a jet crash in New Jersey. As we talked about accidents, he said, "Do you know what I'd do if any of my children were killed in an accident? I'd sue and collect money. You could collect enough money to buy a farm." We told him that would not be turning the other cheek as the Bible teaches us. He said, "The Bible also teaches an eye for an eye and a tooth for a tooth." We just smiled and kept further opinions to ourselves. After he dropped us off, he again thanked us for the Boston cream pie and said he'll be back again some day for more.

Now, on the morning of our son's funeral, someone who we had only met once came back with a card of sympathy. It touched us deeply. And our young nephew who had a life-threatening disease is still living and seems to be cured, while our healthy little boy was snatched away from us in an instant. Who can pretend to fathom the mysteries of life and death?

The day of the funeral was a beautiful sunny day. Several hundred people attended. The funeral was held up in the barn, where the floors had been swept and carpets had been laid.

As we waited to cross the road, traffic kept coming. My thoughts lingered at the spot where Junior's shoe and sock were found. Probably we were crossing right at the spot where he had been hit. Would I ever get used to this? We walked up the barn hill behind his dear body, which was carried in the coffin by two of his cousins and two men who were our former hired boys. As we walked into the barn I thought of the many times we had walked in there for other purposes: unloading hay, playing hide-and-seek, and much more. In this same barn Junior had played in every nook and cranny with his brothers.

Could this be real? It seemed I was in a trance. When were we going to wake up and discover this was all only a dream? It reminded me very much of that falling sensation you experience in your dreams sometimes. You are powerless to stop yourself from hitting the earth, however hard you try. Then you wake up and discover it was only a dream. What a relief! But there is a vast difference in these two dreams. This time we wake up and discover this is all too true.

People had gathered from the area and from neighboring counties. There were Amish, non-Amish, and Mennonites. They had all pitched in to help in the past weeks at two accident scenes. Many were here who could not understand the German sermon. We appreciated the presence of them all.

The sermon was very touching and fitting. We especially liked how the minister explained the story in the Bible about the young boy who had a small basket of food. There was a multitude of 5,000 people gathered to hear Jesus speak, and His disciples were worried about feeding them. After Jesus blessed the food, it was enough to feed the whole multitude! Then the minister added, "Here lies a young boy who has fed many, many people by his death, in a spiritual sense." What a nice thought! We were deeply moved. Our dear little boy who was always so unselfish. It is very fitting that he could touch so many lives. A life so brief, yet his mission on earth was fulfilled. We found out how many lives were touched in the following months.

The minister also mentioned how Jesus loved to stop by the house of Lazarus, Mary, and Martha. That also made me weep as I tried to reason, "If Jesus likes to stop by here to pick flowers from our house, then we want to accept it, however hard it is." Those ministers cannot realize how much those sermons meant to us. Many words of comfort were shared.

After the services, everyone filed past the casket for one last view of David, Jr. All was very quiet. This time his body was carried out of the barn to a waiting team and carriage. The teams of horses and buggies were all numbered, then hitched up and lined in order for all who intended to join the close relatives to the cemetery. We had to wait because of traffic. Trucks went by and made several horses rear up. The traffic was a typical scene to us but seemed very out of place in a time like this. Many who saw it had not realized the amount of traffic that travels past our place.

We had twelve miles to the cemetery which is located in a quiet spot along a country road. One almost hated to drive in, disturbing the tranquility of the scene before us. We were consumed with memories of ten years ago, traveling the same path to lay our son Johnnie to rest. The sun shone brightly as we gathered in the cemetery. The casket was opened one last time for all to have a last look at David, Jr. Our three sons just gazed at him for awhile, as we stood beside them. One's gaze could just linger—afraid to stop looking. Knowing you'll just **have** to let go, yet wishing to hold on forever.

There have been times when little Emma stayed with in-laws for a few days. We missed her, yet we were never engulfed in a deep loneliness, as we always fully expected her to come home again. That was no comparison to this parting!

Now as we stood by Junior's body for the last time, I tried to instill in my mind every feature of his dear face. And it seemed as if I **must** see his clear blue eyes open once more. A painful lump formed in my throat. We **had** to let him go. With a deep inward sigh, I tried to release him. I suddenly realized that time is not to be comprehended by us humans. One day your loved one is with you and so soon life is over. Truly, this life is even as a vapor, a passing flower, as the Psalmist writes. This separation would be forever on this earth, and we had no control to shorten or lengthen that time. It left my body weak. I simply could not comprehend that this would be our last opportunity to see our beloved child in this life.

My emotions seemed to have reached their limits. Oh, how I wished to go with him! It would seem like a release from this now painful world. Once more I stroked his forehead and blond hair. "Oh, gentle one, how we'll miss you!" David whispered, "Bye-bye, Junior boy." The numbed mind accepts the fact that it's our last physical connection with Junior, and it's the beginning of a heart-rending separation. We could actually feel the "arms of Love" surrounding us, supporting us. On our own we would collapse.

We were now once again a fragmented family picking up pieces. The lid on the casket was shut, and we realized we would never again see his dear face on this earth. I felt faint. Would this nightmare never end? We gave him up in quiet acceptance. Truly, "our loss was his gain!" He was laid in a newly dug grave beside the spot where his brother was buried. Jacob squatted down to read the epitaph on his twin brother's tombstone. I wondered what his thoughts were.

Some verses were read aloud. The minister who read them also said, "I have to think, one less person to come to church; one less little hand to shake Sunday mornings." That touched us. Before the people parted, there was a time of silent prayer. It was, oh, so quiet. In the stillness one had to wonder who would be the next one to be laid in this graveyard. Many blessings and words of comfort were shared with us. Suddenly I was really ready to leave this place. I could not see Junior's face anymore, and the mound of soil seemed almost like a mockery.

We were a tired and emotionally drained family as we drove the twelve miles home. I kept thinking of Junior and how happy he must be. That thought gave me much comfort.

In mourning, there is nothing more bitter and sweet at the same time than the thought of a beloved child now an angel in Heaven. This most precious thought will be a great comfort to us, if the time comes when we are on our deathbed, knowing these two sons are awaiting us and are safe in the arms of Jesus. We still did not miss Junior. Subconsciously, we kept thinking, "He'll come back ." Only months later did we really miss him.

The painful hours grew into painful days and then into months. Our lives and routines changed, along with our perspective of life in general. I read somewhere, "Never bury the body of your loved one before accepting resurrection in return." With that, life was bearable.

As we drove home we had a lot of time to think. There was one less child in our carriage, one less joyful voice. I remembered the feelings of depression I had experienced after returning from Johnnie's burial. We had left a part of ourselves in that grave. I tried to ward off those feelings. As we drove in our driveway, one of the men in our church met us to unhitch our team. What a warm feeling! But he also greeted us with the tragic news that our neighbor's five-year-old son had been killed just after we left for the burial. He had been driven over by a skid loader and instantly killed.

Along with all our relatives who had come for supper, we went right over to their farm a half mile up the road. We wept and shared sympathy with them. Few words were said. Early Friday morning the deacon in our church came and said, "I came to do your work so you can go to the funeral." How very thoughtful!

We attended five-year-old Roger Martin's funeral. It was almost like a replica of Junior's funeral two days before, and the tears flowed even more. How we hurt with that family!

Chapter 10

Difficulty In Parting

A few days after the accident Corporal Ramos came out to talk with us, and several officers came to do a drag test of the skid marks on the road. They found 144 feet of skid marks.

As the days went by, there were many feelings to deal with. One feeling is a special sensitivity to happiness and laughter following the death of a loved one. I thought of the driver of the car and could only imagine what feelings he must be dealing with. Though David had not seen or met him yet, we hoped the driver would be able to come soon.

One evening his parents brought him for a visit. We did our best to make it easy for him. We all talked about other things, but I felt it would be better if we talked about the accident. I asked him what he saw and how it actually happened.

The driver said he saw all four boys beside the road on both sides. Then he saw the smallest one start to cross the road. If the boy would have kept going, he would have been fine. But as he crossed the center line, he suddenly stopped. He saw the car approaching, turned around, and ran back. The driver said he slammed on the brakes, but could not stop in time.

We could well imagine Junior as he suddenly saw the approaching car, then panicked. It immediately made me feel bad, thinking he "knew" he would be hit and having a time of fear, however brief it was. That thought hurt deeply. But David said that made him feel better, knowing he didn't just run out from behind the shed, onto the road (as we had feared), just as if he had not been taught better. Also, the fact that he stopped, and then turned around shows he had an appointment. One can see it as the guiding hand of God from that perspective.

Now, I had come to the realization that Junior had had a short time of fear before he died. I really struggled to accept that at first, even as I imagined that stark feeling of fear, had I been in that position. From experience, we know how easy it is to nearly step out on the road, only to see a speeding car coming over the hill. In reality, we know it would have been only a few seconds of fright. But I've relived those few seconds with Junior many, many times. One could think, "Why trouble yourself with thoughts like that?" But it is so normal. We are so human; we think we need a reason for all things, and are also inclined to think we need to understand why these things happen.

At some point we must confront our endless reasonings, and we need to try and think as we read in Isaiah 55, "'My thoughts are not your thoughts, nor my ways your ways,' says the Lord. 'For as the Heavens are higher than the earth, so are my ways higher than your ways and my thoughts than your thoughts....'" Then our faith steps in, but even that sometimes failed. The question often arose within me, "What is faith?" I concluded that it is something we believe in, even when we cannot see it. Sometimes the way is so dark. Then that "belief" within us enables us to see the Light again.

I had mentioned how easy it is to step out on the road, and so soon a car can be upon you. I realize that from experience. This happened to me a week after the accident and it left me badly shaken. A big truck, called a hammer-mill, was at our farm to grind corn for dairy feed. It comes weekly, doing custom grinding for a lot of farmers. This operation creates a lot of noise. The owner of this business had sent us a picnic ham a few days after Junior's death, so I went to give the driver a thank-you note to deliver to the person responsible for that kind gesture. I looked in each direction before I crossed the road. I could not depend on my hearing since it was too noisy with the hammer-mill in operation.

I still don't know why I didn't see a vehicle coming. It may have been my line of vision; perhaps two cars had been passing each other in opposite directions just then, and I had failed to see the one car, or perhaps I had been simply too preoccupied to notice. Nevertheless, when I was in the middle of the road I happened to glance down the road. What I saw nearly caused my heart to stop! A red van was almost upon me. Instinctively, I dashed for the other side and I did not stop running until I was in the cow stable. There I collapsed on the curb, shaking all over.

Like a flash, the scene of Junior's accident leaped before me. I felt it could just as easily have been me. The only difference was that Junior had "frozen" in his tracks while I quickly ran. Also, this van was traveling slowly. I felt I simply could not live like this anymore. In desperation I called the police barracks and asked to talk with

Trooper Bittner. He wasn't there at the time, but the lady at the desk said she would have him call back as soon as he came in. I don't know what I figured he could do to change the situation I was in. Perhaps I needed reassurance.

Soon the phone rang and it was Trooper Bittner. He wondered what he could do for me. Briefly I told him what happened. I said, "I feel as if I'm in a trap and I can't live like this anymore. What are we supposed to do?"

His response was, "What would you do if you lived beside a river and one of your children drowned in it?"

I said, "I guess we'd move away."

He then asked, "Where would you move to? Would you move to another home and find yourself beside another river?" He kindly told me they would be out and keep an eye on the traffic as much as possible. That reassurance calmed me somewhat. His questions were thought provoking. They were new thoughts to me as I pondered over them. I knew he meant that we could move to another location that could be equally as dangerous.

*   *   *

Many times at night I had trouble sleeping. As I heard cars speed by, I'd only see dear Junior, so innocent, being struck, and what an impact it must have been! It haunts me to think he was a victim of such violence. He, who was so far removed, so utterly detached from anything violent. It did not seem fair! I'd try to remove such thoughts, but they kept returning, somewhat like a nagging headache.

Then my thoughts lingered on the thin thread between life and death. It is, oh, so thin and can be severed in an instant. But when does the spirit leave the body? When the heartbeats cease? No, even after a heart has stopped beating, it can be started again with new medical techniques. And hearts can be transplanted into other humans—but you can't transplant the soul. I've concluded that it could be in the brain. But again, pieces of the brain can be removed by surgery. I've finally come to the conclusion that it will always remain a mystery to us and beyond human understanding; however, it leaves much to ponder upon.

It would have seemed right to see Junior wave good-bye as he was leaving. But we have nothing to say to that, however close our heartstrings were attached.

A few days after the funeral I felt I must feel some contact with Junior. I thought of his clothes drawer, the only drawer he could call his own. The other boys had drawers of their own where they stored all kinds of personal objects—oddities such as seashells, empty gum wrappers, and things that boys collect. I had planned to empty another drawer in the desk for Junior to store his collectibles. But, in the meantime, he kept his little treasures in his clothes drawer. As I thought of that I went to see what treasures I could find. There, neatly tucked under his shirts was a small pile of treasures. I sat down and wept. There were two balloons, a homemade bookmarker, a pencil, a small stick-on seal, and a pack of chewing gum with one piece of gum, torn into eighteen small bits.

The gum spoke of Junior's unselfish nature. His grandpa had given it to him the week before, and when he opened the pack, his little sister had kept begging him for gum. I saw him tear it apart and whenever she came begging for more, Junior would give her a small piece. Of course she always swallowed it. Finally, in frustration, he told me she'll eat all his gum, so he put it into his drawer.

Junior had received the stick-on seal from his brother Jacob the week before as a reward for pulling the lawn mower with baler twine while Jacob pushed. I remember their happy smiles as they came indoors and ran upstairs where his brother gave him the seal, which he had received in school. Junior's face beamed as he put his treasure away.

Again, I was reminded how it's the little and simple things in life that bring the most pleasure. One can truly appreciate and enjoy the little, everyday things or events in life when one has been shown directly that things and people in this life are not measured by their greatness. These "great" things and "great" people can be snatched away from us in a moment, and we mortals have no control over it. Even King Solomon, with all his great wisdom, lamented his great wealth and riches.

One day I asked the boys, "What shall we do with Junior's dishes and toys?"

They didn't know. Now Junior's things are still on display with the other boys' valuables. They wondered about his penny bank. One of them said Junior had four one-dollar bills. I told them they could divide the money. Junior would want them to have it. They brought down his precious penny bank and divided it among our four remaining children.

When Junior was only a few days old, his namesake, David E. Huyard, had given him a one-hundred dollar bill as a gift. I promised the boys we would divide that money among them and Emma, and start a bank account for them. That pleased them very much.

One day I went to the bank and told the teller that I wanted to start bank accounts for each of our children. She took me to a small room and explained the procedure of starting new accounts. She then asked the names of our children. Before I realized it, I also mentioned Junior's name with the rest. I corrected my mistake, and then broke down and told this stranger what had happened. She was a sympathetic listener; it helped me through the rest of that day. Somehow, dividing Junior's $100.00 among the children brought me much comfort. It was something they would always remember.

Another obstacle to face was the need to clean out his drawer. It remained untouched for eight months. Sometimes I'd open his drawer just to see his shirts and pants again. It kept his memory alive. Finally, one day I went through all his clothes and stored some. Others I gave away. A five-year-old cousin of Junior's got his tattered straw hat. Every time I see him, I can see Junior's face peering from under it. One grasps to keep any possible memory alive, for you fear if you lose memories, you lose everything.

When your life has been shattered by a tragedy that has attracted public attention, you discover "getting out" is one of the hardest experiences you'll ever encounter, though you are often urged to do just that. One wants to remain in familiar surroundings, because they still bear the imprint of the absent one. Finally, you come to realize that, too, is vacant. But it is too painful to go meet people. It is too much effort to get dressed to go away. The list goes on.... But there is no need to rush yourself.

If you are given enough time, you will be able to struggle against the tide again. When you are urged by others to "go away" in order to get your mind away from your tragedy, it only shows you how quickly life returns to normal for others, while life never returns to normal for you. You appreciate it when you do not feel pushed by others to go out and be among people. Sometimes people mean it well by urging you to go visiting, adding, "It will be good for you."

We know from experience that that approach has the wrong effect on grieving people. By trying to force yourself to forget your tragedy, you are only denying that it happened. You will need to face up to it, and it takes longer for some than others. There is no "set time" limit. The best someone can do to help you through rough times is to be understanding and helpful. It is just as important to be understanding and patient with people who suddenly face a sickness, or whose child may be stricken with an illness or other affliction or trial in life.

At first when I'd think of Junior, I'd think of him with tongue in cheek, coloring away diligently, or of him sitting on the rocker, singing, often until his tired head dropped and he'd doze on the chair. I'd gaze at his dear face and wonder what will become of him yet.

I'd immediately snuff out those memories by hoeing weeds in the garden. I dived into work as an eraser for painful memories, rather than attacking them head-on from the start. I felt I could never survive it if I faced up to it entirely. If I blocked my mind from memories of Junior I would not feel the pain as much. If I sat down and concentrated on thinking of him, the longing to see him became so great and the pain so intense that it was more than I could endure. I felt I could escape the pain by not thinking of him. Was I trying to escape reality?

Only the following winter did I realize and understand some of my feelings. Instead of going through grief, I tried to go around it. Eventually, I needed to go through it, and the longer I waited, the harder it became.

We can live in a life of pretense only so long. All summer I had been content to think only of Junior's gain and his happiness. I thought of how happy he must be and was so thankful his wish was fulfilled. In the bleakness of the winter months reality hit me, and I missed him terribly. Many times I felt I'd gladly walk a thousand miles simply to see him again, and to hold him close. The longing to see him and feel his dear hugs threatened to overpower me. I felt I could not discuss it with anyone, as they wouldn't understand after all these months. After parting with a child the second time, I developed a feeling of insecurity. I was afraid of becoming too attached to anyone. I feared losing what, or whom, I loved. I loved my many friends, but I did not trust close friendships, for fear of partings. Partings are hard.

Chapter 11

There's Danger on the Road

How were our children feeling all this time?

Two weeks after the funeral, we were at the viewing of a little boy who had died of cancer. The boys did not want to go in to view this child, so we did not force them. David was holding Emma, who was almost twenty-one months old. As soon as she saw the little boy in the coffin, she said aloud, and in very plain words, "Dat iss da Junior!" (There is Junior.) It shocked us both. We realized that the last memory she had of him was as he lay in his coffin. She must have missed him greatly. The same day after we returned home, she went out the back door and called him by name. It was heartbreaking. We tried to explain where he went and then she'd look toward the door, almost as if she expected him to come in anytime. Just what were her thoughts?

The week following the accident, I noticed there were two extra pillows on Jacob's bed. I asked him why he wanted more pillows. He hesitated a little and then said, "Because it just seems as if someone is laying against me." I told him he could have all the pillows he wanted.

Amos did not want to be left alone anywhere. He did not want to go to the barn alone anymore or go upstairs in the house. We never forced him to do either one, realizing it will take time and patience on his part as well as ours. We were inclined to become very protective of the rest of our children. We almost clung to them. We were afraid "not to" for fear of losing them, too. It seemed I was obsessed with the need to know where ALL our children were at all times. Yet it was difficult to do and often seemed like a crushing weight which was too heavy to carry. It was almost at the point where it seemed to irritate the children at times.

We would often remind the children to be careful in whatever they were doing or wherever they went. One day when Jacob was riding his scooter, I said to him, "Now **please** be careful. Just stay away from the road!"

So quickly he said, "It's not my fault Junior was killed."

I was taken completely by surprise and shaken up. I tried to explain to him. "No, we do not feel it was your fault Junior was killed, but we are only trying to protect the rest of you because we still want you very much." That incident gave us an insight into the boys' feelings.

After the accident we noticed state police cars often parked down by the crossroads and also in our front yard. They were using radar to check for speeding traffic.

At first I didn't like to see a patrol car pull in, but after a while that changed. We became dependent upon them. Each time a patrol car came, it gave us a warm feeling. They had no idea what a source of comfort it was just to know they cared enough to try to slow down traffic.

Trooper Bittner lived in Manheim at the time and passed by us on his way to and from work. We watched for his wave or listened for the toot of his horn as he'd go by. His wave helped us through many a dreary day.

About two weeks after the accident Trooper Bittner came in his patrol car and said he'd like to talk to the boys. He said he needed to complete his report about the accident and wanted to question each one of them.

Trooper Bittner took off his police hat and squatted down beside them at their level. He said, "I know this is going to be difficult for you, but I need to know what you saw and heard."

Samuel whispered in my ear, "Why does he need to know?"

He did not want to talk about the accident.

When Trooper Bittner was finished, I mentioned to him the constant worry of the safety of our children.

He said to me, "You can only do the best you can and leave the rest up to a Higher Hand."

As he watched the children on the swing, he remarked, "These children are loved. They have a mother and dad who care about them."

At the time that comment struck me as a little absurd. Of course we love our children! Later I decided people in his profession probably see some children who are not loved.

He then asked the boys, "Would you like to see the police barracks?"

Their faces lit up and they beamed as they nodded their heads.

— *Chapter 12* —

Facing Life Again

On July 8, Trooper Bittner picked us all up and took us to the Ephrata State Police Barracks for a tour. He showed us each room and explained each of their duties. The boys were especially impressed by a poster on the wall showing many patrol cars with a state trooper beside each car. The poster featured the abuse of alcohol. He later gave this poster to the boys, which really pleased them.

He showed us how fingerprinting is done and took all their finger prints, put them on files, and gave them to the boys.

After he brought us home we sat on the porch and had a snack while we visited and watched the traffic go by. It was a special day for us all to remember.

Sometime in June a state trooper parked beside the heifer pen by the road. He asked if it was offensive to us if he parked there.

I said, "Not at all."

It was a good place to check speeds with radar, being obscured from the traffic. We had never met this trooper before. He introduced himself as Joe Christaldi and was very faithful in checking speeds with radar, keeping the speed of cars under control. It is a delight to the children every time he comes. To this day he still comes almost once a week. We will always remember his kindness and helpfulness. Those state troopers played a major role in the healing of grief for us and the children, and we will always have a warm spot in our hearts for them.

The weather was exceptionally rainy that summer, and frequent rains dampened our spirits and magnified our grief.

One rainy Monday morning, Trooper Bittner stopped by on his way home from the night shift. We talked for several hours as we drank coffee. I had some questions concerning the accident that I had always wanted to ask him. It was the first time David and I talked freely with him about Junior's death. It felt good to be able to ask him anything that was on our minds.

Before he left we thanked him for his help and told him he had no idea how much his visits meant to us and we hoped he would continue to come. He told us he was only too glad to be a "vehicle to healing." I liked that expression. After he left, both David and I were moved to tears and I pondered why he seemed so special to us. Were we guilty of clinging to any thread connected to the last moments Junior was here with us and still not "letting go?" I eventually decided it was not only that; we felt a sincere friendship from someone who had also experienced partings and pain.

I believe anyone who has experienced heartaches in their life has a love to reach out to others in need. They will also be quicker to notice such needs; it is part of the good which comes from tragedy. The circle widens as we need new friends. People become your friends, not by choice, but by circumstances you did not choose. Tears of sympathy come easily while hearing of others who have experienced pain. One would want to protect others from heartaches, but they are inevitable in this life. It is only endurable by the grace of God and caring people who are actually angels unaware.

It was impossible to continue in life and pretend that our dear child had never existed. He was loved so dearly and was so much a part of our daily life. It is because of the deep love we had for him that we often weep, and one does not "want" to forget. One can hardly become callous in the face of death if we keep our eyes and hearts on the "Giver of life." I even get the feeling that we might become callous if death would not intervene at times in this busy world of materialism. How else would we long for a better world than this one? The longing to leave this world for that Beautiful Land only increases as time goes by.

*   *   *

As a family, we love to sing together, especially on Sunday forenoons at home. One Sunday forenoon about three months after Junior's death, David suggested that we sing. It was the first time we had tried to sing since May. We sang a few songs, but the words seemed to stick in my throat. I could sense it in the others, too. Very naturally, someone chose Junior's favorite song, "Just a Little While to Stay Here." As we sang I noticed it became quieter and when I looked up, Samuel burst into tears and ran into the next room. He lay on the sofa and shook with sobs. Jacob went upstairs and cried on his bed. Needless to say, that put an end to singing. We wept with the boys. I asked Samuel if singing reminded him of Junior. He nodded and said, "I wish so much he had not died!" He said he just couldn't understand why Junior had to go. Jacob did not say much, but I think just talking about it made them feel better.

Another Sunday only a few weeks later, when all was quiet in the house, we heard the distant screeching of tires. So quickly one of the boys said, "I just **hate** that sound." They all agreed. Then I asked them if they would tell me what they saw and heard at the time of the accident. They all cried as they told me freely what happened as they saw it. It was the first time we had ever questioned them or heard them tell their own story, aside from seeing the police report.

The boys said that Samuel was in the corn crib writing notes for their second treasure hunt and Junior sat on the steps watching him. Junior was delivering the notes. Samuel told him to take a note to the mailbox, which Junior did. Just then Jacob and Amos stopped by and asked if they were ready. They weren't, so Jacob and Amos left again and started around the barn beside the road on their scooters. Then Samuel said to Junior, "That was the wrong note. Go get that note in the mailbox and put this one in."

A few minutes later Samuel heard tires screech. He ran out the door and saw a car hit Junior. Junior was carried about seventy-five feet on the car. As soon as he fell off, Samuel and Amos ran over to Junior. Jacob and Amos had also heard the tires and then a bump, and looked around and saw Junior fall off.

Samuel and Amos asked Junior, "Are you all right, Junior?" They both said they saw him move his eyes and his one hand. This was the first I had heard this and I very much wanted to hear every detail. What may have seemed unimportant to the casual listener was very important to me—those last seconds of his life. I also realized it was good for the boys to talk about it. Samuel said he thinks when Junior moved his hand, that was when an angel came and took his hand.

Amos had his own version. He said he thinks Junior was waving "bye-bye" to them. What precious thoughts! Jacob only wept and said he just can't get over the fact that he did not go over to Junior. He said he was afraid to go to him. He had been like me. He cried harder as he said, "I just **stand** it that I didn't go see him one last time before the ambulance took him away." Of course, Jacob had no way of

51

knowing that Junior would not come home again alive, even though I had warned him this might happen. That did not sink in. You do not plan these things, so neither can you plan how you would react in any similar crisis.

I think a certain amount of guilt will always follow the death of a child, but it only results in disturbing any peace of mind concerning his death. Why didn't we keep better watch over him at all times? The continuous flow of traffic is so unnerving. Can you imagine the full-time job you would have, living under these circumstances, feeling that you need to watch every child every minute of each day? Are we putting our family in jeopardy by living like this when we know we all need to daily cross this busy road? The latter question often haunts me. We can be as careful as possible but it is still dangerous. At the same time, the fact remains that we are not in control of all things.

Where does God's will and His plan come in? We realize how futile it is to try and plan the life span of our children and ourselves. When God calls us home, it doesn't matter what we are doing. We cannot prevent it unless He wills it so. That was shown to us ten years ago when our child died in his crib, quite undisturbed by any humans. From that perspective, we have some peace of mind concerning Junior's death.

Chapter 13

Struggling For Survival

After Junior's death I thought of the scare we had just a week before. Evening was approaching but it was not yet dark when I asked Junior if he would fetch some tea leaves out by the fence between the garden and the meadow. I told him we wanted to have a tea party that evening and he cheered about that. I gave him a small knife, and he was gone. After a while I wondered what was taking him so long; by then darkness had fallen.

I went to the meadow to see if he was playing. He wasn't around. I called and called him and walked all around the surrounding area. When he did not answer, I became somewhat alarmed. I went to the barn and asked if anyone had seen Junior. No one had. The hired man and Jacob went down to the creek to look, and across the road. We all called him and I felt a rising panic within me. I went into the house again and called him. Finally, I went upstairs thinking maybe he was asleep. There he was, sitting on the bed beside one of his brothers who was showing him his collection of stones. What a relief! I asked him why he didn't answer when we called him. He looked so innocently at me and said calmly, "I didn't know you were looking for me." He had simply been sidetracked by his brother. I hugged him and said, "Let's go now and make tea." It was an episode that really showed me how much we as parents care about and cling to our children.

Now when I feel I **must** find him again and bring him back to us, I can only picture him as perfectly serene and calm wherever he is, reminding me, "It's all right, Mother." He taught me so much in his five years. He possessed such a trusting and enduring nature at which we often marveled. When I would become frustrated about anything I would only have to look at him, and his trusting blue eyes always affected me in a calming way. Now all that is gone, but we try to remember what we all gained by his years with us.

The seasons changed, yet we were hardly aware of it. We struggled for survival in a world that had become wearisome. Things we used to enjoy and love to do now did not interest us. A mother who lost a child made the comment one day that she feels as if she is ten years older. We can relate to that feeling very well. I believe it is the suddenness of it all, changing your thinking and your normal routine in life. In this fast-paced world, nothing speaks of peace and release. Then I would think of Junior in that Beautiful Land and the glory he now has. In comparison to that, our life on this earth seemed so worthless and meaningless.

Your thoughts are on the Great Beyond. You pause for long moments to view a pretty sunset or sunrise, and marvel at the exquisite beauty of it. It reminds you of Heaven. You try to imagine the angels, the streets of gold, and the pearly gates. If we marvel at the scenes of beauty on this earth—how much more beautiful must the other side be! It seems drudgery to get up in the morning and start another day. These activities seem so empty when you compare them to Junior's bliss. You experience such a chronic tiredness that leaves you exhausted in body and in mind.

I believe we all know the feeling of waking up tired in the morning at times and being tired for the rest of the day. We need only to remind ourselves that tomorrow or the following day we will feel better. Usually a good night's sleep restores our energy, but this is a type of tiredness which no amount of sleep can quench. You wake up equally tired, day after day, for a long time. You get tired of thinking, thinking in endless circles. In the end the fact remains—your loved one will not come back. You must travel on, however hard it is. As the family sits down to eat you involuntarily glance around for that missing person to take his seat. As you leave the house to go to church you hesitate at the door; one more needs to come. There is always that feeling of incompleteness. You finally just learn to live with it.

His memory is our keepsake,
With that we'll never part.
God has him in His keeping;
We have him in our hearts.

When someone asks me how many children we have, it disturbs me. I can't think fast enough to say how many are left. That question has often caught me off guard as I struggled to silently name each child. Then, shall I answer, "We have four children;" or, "We had five;" or, "We would have six if all were living"? My answer mostly depends on who asks the question.

54

— *Chapter 14* —

Not Again!

On November 10 of the same year as Junior's death, we were once more reminded of how utterly helpless we are in circumstances when mishaps occur beyond our control. How very thin this thread of life really is! Six months after Junior's accident another accident occurred that left us shaken. It took me a long while to be able to think rationally of that experience.

That afternoon at 3:30 as I was in the kitchen, I heard the screeching of tires. When I went to the window and looked out I met a scene that filled me with horror beyond words! It was an almost identical scene to Junior's accident and death. The only thing I saw was the body of one of our boys, lying in the gutter by the road. I saw it was Jacob, the oldest. I just stared in total disbelief, waiting for his body to move. He simply did not move! I was oblivious to anything else as I ran out the door and simply cried to heaven, "Oh, God, NO! Please, not again!" Just then someone called up to me, "Go call an ambulance."

I ran to the barn and again dialed 911, but I was hysterical as I tried to give sensible directions. The lady asked me to please calm down and tell her what happened. With difficulty I got the message across and added, "Please hurry!" This seemed so awfully impossible, too soon— too new!

I ran to where Jacob lay and knelt beside him, calling his name. I was almost beside myself! Immediately a lady came up and said, "I checked him and he has a pulse. I'm a registered nurse." I kissed Jacob's cold white face and talked to him again, begging him to squeeze my hand if he heard me. He did not respond.

After about fifteen or twenty minutes, David arrived. He had been in the farthest field, picking corn, when a car stopped beside the road and asked if he was David Smucker. They told him his son had just been hit by a car. David had to surpress feelings of anger and disbelief, just as I had to; however, he had some time to think before he came upon the scene. When he called Jacob by name, he soon started stirring and opened his eyes.

The ambulance arrived and again I told David to go with him and I would come later. The two ambulance drivers were the same ones who had arrived at the scene of Junior's accident. As they walked past me, they just shook their heads. There was so little one could say! Trooper Christaldi arrived, off-duty. He wondered if he should stay with the children. It was then that I thought, "Oh, what are the children thinking?" Amos was crying very hard. He thought his brother was dead.

David went with the ambulance as they headed for the hospital, the same hospital where Junior had been taken only six months earlier. Someone handed me a pocket knife found beside the road. It was the spot where Jacob had lain. My heart cried silently within me, "Oh, please let him be able to use it again!"

Neighbors arrived, one by one, and no one knew what to say; however, I sensed their sympathy. I was filled with anxiety the next hour since I did not know the extent of his injuries. I learned afterwards that within that first hour several prayer chains had already begun. Many, many prayers were sent to the throne of God on Jacob's behalf. God must have heard the pleadings.

Two neighbor women arrived to stay with the children, and brought supper. Trooper Bittner arrived, also off-duty, and took me to the hospital. I do not remember what I said on the way in to the hospital, but the trooper may have been shocked as I gave vent to my feelings. I expressed myself as I did because I knew I could trust him. I told him I felt I was losing my trust in God and couldn't even pray. I will always remember his answer. He said, "If you feel you are losing your faith and can't pray, then just read the Word of God. Let that do it for you. Read the Psalms."

Neighbors arrived and did our chores. It made me weak to think of how dependent we were upon these people.

When we saw Jacob in his bed in the hospital, he gave us a weak smile. He had a concussion and bruises on his forehead and knee. We came home from the hospital late that night. He stayed two days.

Our son's life had been spared. We felt that this time a car had been sent to save his life. It was a freak accident and no one will ever know what really happened. Jacob fell from a gravity bin wagon while going down the road, and landed on the hood of a passing car just as it was parallel with the wagon. A second sooner he would have landed in front of the car, and one can only guess what would have been the outcome of that. Was this only a coincidence? We battled with a variety of thoughts over the following weeks. Probably the hardest struggle was accepting the fact that we again needed to deal with outsiders who were involved in the accident through no fault of their own. They were hurting, too.

Early the next morning our minister came over and wept with us. He said they had heard the news at midnight upon returning home from a wedding. He told us, "I prayed earnestly for you." What a comfort! He also counseled us not to base our feelings too much on these accidents and make any quick decisions because of them. He related other incidents of how people had had similar experiences in succession and how they survived. This was revealed to us more clearly as time went on.

*   *   *

One day a car drove in and someone came to our door. I recognized him as our former milk truck driver whom we had not seen for several years. His wife was also along. He was a fine Christian and we missed him when he did not come anymore. At first we talked of other things, but I felt he did not stop just for small talk. After a bit he said he learned of our son's death and wondered it it would be too painful to talk about. He wanted to know how and what happened. I told them briefly about the accident, and our conversation drifted to the depth of life and death. I then shared with him Junior's conversation three days prior to his death and what a comfort that was. He asked if they might give me a hug, and with tears in his eyes he said, "Thank you for sharing. Such stories are an inspiration to me and only strengthen my faith."

I was equally moved but felt the situation was reversed. They were an inspiration to me on the evening of a very warm summer day, and my soul was refreshed by another caring person. This was an important lesson to me. Not only was it good for me to talk about it; it also taught me that good can come by sharing if we are not too selfish to do so. Too often we are prone to carry a burden alone, needlessly. It takes so little. I had to ask the question, "Do I sense the needs of others when they need strength and prayers of other people?"

People who have traumatic experiences will often indulge in something "extra" for comfort or for a crutch. Some may binge on food; some may sleep excessively; some spend many sleepless nights and depend on coffee during the daytime as a small source of comfort.

I'm afraid I fell into the latter category. I increased from one cup of coffee a day to several cups; then I spent many nights awake for half the night. But I discovered there is even good in that. Sleepless nights are my quiet times in prayer. It is a good time to commune with God.

— Chapter 15 —

The Christmas Spirit

December 19th was a chilly Saturday. That particular forenoon David, the children, and I went to the cemetery to place the tombstone by Junior's grave. Now there stood two tombstones, side by side, and our thoughts went Heavenward as we thought of our two angels. Our thoughts were way beyond the graves. It was a quiet ceremony for us and we did not linger long. The children did not say much and neither did we, but we all felt deeply. We had crossed another obstacle.

As Christmas approached it seemed that tension mounted in our family. Where was the usual enthusiasm, the singing of carols, the joy of telling the children the story of Christ's birth? It was all a forced ordeal. I thought of a year ago and how Junior had enjoyed all those things so much. One memory is especially clear to me and always brings tears when I think of it. Some of my brothers and sisters and their children were here the day after Christmas. Some gifts were exchanged, and my sister-in-law gave Junior a pack of magic markers as a gift. His face just **beamed** as he exclaimed, "Is this for me? You mean for **me**?" He could hardly believe his good fortune.

I cannot forget that incident, and it still smites me a bit in my heart at the memory of it. Is that how much something "new" meant to him?

As this first Christmas without him approached, the realization hit us. There will be one less eager-faced child to watch in enjoyment opening his gifts. The nearer the day came, the bigger the lump formed in my throat as I felt myself becoming more preoccupied and sad. David was the same way. I was not really prepared to ward off the type of feelings I actually had to deal with on Christmas eve.

After everyone was in bed and all was quiet, I tried to shut off my thoughts and anticipate the morrow with the same eagerness the boys had when they went to bed—with big smiles and, "we'll be up early!" I hoped I was able to feign happiness in spite of the acute feeling of loneliness and sadness which engulfed me. I tried to sleep but sleep would not come. The clock showed 12:30 and I was still awake. I did not want to be caught in self-pity so I centered my thoughts on widows, homeless, and hungry people. Tears flowed silently.

The next morning as I went to the barn to help milk, I watched the stars. Again I wondered at the vast beyond and imagined the feelings of the shepherds so many years ago who witnessed that wonderful and awesome sight of the angels in the sky, proclaiming Christ's birth! Their thoughts had been turned Heavenward just as mine now were. Were those hosts of angels at one time some parents' little boys and girls? Or were those angels who had been created since the beginning of time? Needless to say, I thought of our two angels in Heaven. How I longed to see them!

As I joined David in the cow stable, I said to him wearily, "It seems I just can't get the Christmas spirit." His response was, "Today it is seven months that Junior left us." I was too weary and heartsick to reply. I helped with the chores and went back to the house. Again I silently wept. Where, oh where was my joy at the thought of Junior's happiness? Why couldn't I feel that now? And why do we weep? It is because of that great love parents have for their children, and they become so lonesome for them when they leave, never to return. Children are our most prized possessions, and we love them dearly! I knew we would treasure ours even more now.

When I came to the house the lights were on and Jacob greeted me with a "Merry Christmas, Mom." He was followed by Samuel and Amos, who asked me if I know what Merry Christmas means. They said it sounds like "Mary kiss me." I told them, "Okay, for that you'll each get a kiss!"

It turned out to be a special day in spite of the sadness. Again, the state troopers came to our rescue! At 7:30 that morning Trooper Bittner stopped by on his way home from night shift and joined us for breakfast. The boys made the statement, "Breakfast lasts forever." We finally finished our coffee and all sang together, "Joy to the World." Then each received his gifts. To our surprise and the children's delight, Trooper Bittner gave each of the children a beautifully wrapped package. Emma was positively in awe as she opened her package containing a baby doll with clothes and toys. The stars shown bright in her eyes.

Later in the day, Trooper Christaldi stopped by and gave us an apple pie. He told us he made the pie himself. That pie would have been delicious even if it had been burnt! The Lord surely knew what was needed to brighten our day. Who doesn't believe God sends angels in the form of man? My deep heartache continued on to the next day and several days thereafter. It was the saddest Christmas we had ever experienced, aside from 1981.

*   *   *

December was the hardest month. I believe David and I were both in a stage of utter loneliness; grief had reached a climax. The past half-year was taking its toll. Or perhaps it was the approaching of the bleak winter months, before which we seemed defenseless, or some of both. Any approach in battling those feelings did not work, but time still moved on. Slowly we came to grips with the realization that life **will** continue without our loved one. The full impact of this never hits a person until much later than the actual parting.

— Chapter 16 —

Spring Always Follows Winter

One day in January I saw a scene that touched me. It had snowed the day before, and the earth was covered with a beautiful blanket of snow. The scenery was breathtaking! Early that morning I went to scatter the coal ashes from our stove. There in the garden, in the fresh snow, were the perfect imprints of two angels—wings spread. As I gazed at them, I thought of our two angels in Heaven. When I came to the house I asked the boys if they had made those angels in the snow and they said they had. I did not question why and they did not explain.

As February arrived, our thoughts returned to an incident of a year ago. Three months before Junior's death we went to the viewing of a seven-year-old boy who died after a life-long struggle with liver problems. Of all our boys we only took Junior. As we viewed the body of this little boy, Junior stood beside us and just gazed at him quietly. It seemed he just could not keep his eyes off this little boy whose eyes were shut. He did not say a word as he stood by the coffin for a long time. After a while, the father of the deceased child picked up Junior and held him and talked to him; still, Junior did not say a word, but only looked.

When we were ready to leave I couldn't find Junior. I went to the room where the coffin was and there he stood, all alone in the room, by the side of this little body. Later we were told how others noticed a little boy standing alone by the coffin when they went in to view the body.

I have often wondered what his thoughts were. Had I known what lay ahead I would have questioned him. As it was, he had looked so "at peace" while looking at that little boy, never questioning us about him or his death. Just what had his thoughts been? We will never know. Only three months later he also lay in a coffin, and those parents came to view him and attended his funeral.

61

Spring arrived late in 1993. In a sense we were glad, since we had neither the energy nor the willpower to dive into work that spring. As I mowed the lawn beside the road each week, I would automatically look for the yellow arrow mark on the road, which was clearly visible a year later. It marked the exact spot where Junior had lain beside the road, and it was another daily reminder of him. It seemed I could sense his presence each time I paused to gaze at the spot.

As I unpacked the hummingbird feeders and hung them out in April, I was again reminded of an unusual incident from the previous spring. A few weeks before Junior's death Samuel and Junior ran to me and said they saw a hummingbird! I was a bit skeptical since we had never seen one here before. By their description it sounded as if it truly was one. I peeped around the house and was just in time to see a beautiful hummingbird flit by and fly to the woods. I was completely amazed and in awe. Just the week before I had told the boys I thought I would give a hundred dollars just be be able to see a hummingbird! However, it was the only time we saw one that spring, in spite of our efforts to keep the feeder cleaned and filled. When Junior was killed a week later I had to think of that wee bird. He flew out of our lives and never returned, except in memory.

The day came in March when they had pre-school day at school. The boys were a bit sad as we talked about how Junior now would not go that day. He used to have such a big interest in school and books. After they came home from school that day, the boys said their teacher told them in class, "Now if your brother David would still be living, he would also be here today. But he has a much better Teacher than I am." I asked Samuel if he was glad the teacher said that. He looked so sad as he only nodded his head. It was very thoughtful of her to remember his absence.

How do you answer your remaining children's questions pertaining to death, after the death of one of their siblings? Oh, for wisdom! It is probably a situation that all parents need to face after the painful parting of one of their children. At times you can sense the longings your children are feeling.

One evening a year and a half after Junior's death, my oldest son approached me in the kitchen, his eyes brimming with tears. He said, "Oh, I wish so much my brothers Johnnie and Junior would still be here with us!"

I struggled inwardly for a sensible answer. I told him I often wish so, too. I also asked him why he really wished to have them here. I felt I knew what his answer would be, but I wanted him to express his feelings himself.

He said he thought it would just be more "complete" and so much more fun to all be together. Just then Dad walked in the door and I told him what Jacob had just said. David thought a while before answering, then he said, "Yes, I often think the same thing. I wish they were still here with us, but they will not come back to us. The important thing we want to keep in mind is this: We want to go to them."

With those thoughts ever in mind, we continue on in this present world.

We have been asked numerous times if we don't blame ourselves for tragedies like this, or wonder what we did to deserve it. That is a common and fair question and I am glad to say we were not plagued by such questions. Perhaps we took it as a time of testing concerning our faith; or "for our own good" as quoted in Romans. Also, it could be for the good of others whose lives Junior may have touched in some way. Or, it could have been to draw us closer to God and reconstruct our lives. But we could not see it as "getting even" or "an act of revenge" on God's part. I do not believe He is a vindictive God. We would much rather like to think He loved us enough to chasten us. With such thoughts it is possible to have peace of mind. However, the tempter, the evil one, is always there to try and convince one otherwise, and he attacks when one is weak and tired.

During those winter months I experienced periods of depression which left me drained. I was consumed with loneliness, which probably caused the depression. I am sure plenty of people can relate to such feelings; it is all normal. People grieve differently and in various stages following the death of a loved one. In our family, David's reactions were immediate depression and utter weariness during the first months. He had no interest in his work, and only forced himself from day to day, while I tried to be the resourceful one. Many months later, he kept the family on the level while I struggled for survival.

After all those months when people rarely mentioned Junior's name, I had a strong urge to talk about him, yet I felt too self-conscious to approach the subject to others. Meanwhile, others were probably afraid to mention his name or that subject for fear of hurting me. I try to understand those feelings, realizing there is no ill will intended. But I say this for probably most grieving people: There is nothing more healing than to be able to talk about your loved one. This is very important, and nothing hurts more than when you mention your child's name and wish to talk about him, and are greeted only by silence. An uncomfortable silence. You have the need to talk about him and what happened. This changes with time. To hear his name is the sweetest thing on earth. You also appreciate it when someone tells you what they remember about your child.

The following is a letter from the "Dear Abby" column that appeared in our local morning paper in October 1994. My husband and I both feel that this could be a very insightful message to many persons.

DEAR ABBY: Nine months ago, my husband of 23 years died suddenly and unexpectedly. Although most of my friends have been very helpful, I was appalled by the behavior of many of my acquaintances. They actively avoided me (to the point of ducking in supermarket aisles) for about six months. After that, they acted as if nothing had happened.

I know these people are not purposely cruel. They just didn't know what to say, and now they are afraid to "remind" me of my loss. A simple "I'm so sorry," is all I want to hear—and believe me, the loss is with me all the time. Sometimes I get the impression someone does not know my husband has died, so I tell him or her, only to hear, "Oh, yeah, I read about that."

Abby, all I want is to have my loss acknowledged. Do people fear a scene? The best thing I have ever done is join the Widowed Persons Service sponsored by the AARP and local community organizations. I also joined a bereavement group sponsored by Hospice. Only other widowed people know how I feel and take my feelings seriously. The following appeared in a recent W.P.S. newsletter. I hope you think it is worth printing:

After someone has died, say,...

"What I always liked about ___ was ___."

"I'll never forget the time he and I ___."

"May I take the kids to the beach today?"

"It's OK. Tell me again about ___."

"I just phoned to say hello."

"Tuesday will be a tough day for you. May we spend it together?"

"I thought you might need a hug, or someone to hold your hand today."

"You don't have to hide your tears."

"I love to (trim bushes, etc.). May I do it for you?"

The best thing anybody (who did not know my husband personally) said to me was, "I was so sorry to read about your husband's death. Would you like to talk about it?" *- A widow in New London, Conn.*

When we think of death we do not want to coldly term it as simply "death." We need to think beyond that—it is the door to eternal life. If we would dwell on the deceptive illusion that our loved one simply does not exist any more, then death would have no meaning. We came to terms with the feelings and thoughts of death long ago, and it is not an uncomfortable subject to us. I have often pondered on how to make it easier for others who possibly steer away from it as if it were a plague. Sooner or later, if we live long enough, we will all need to face the death of a loved one. It may be the exception, not the rule, for parents to bury their children. I believe we would admit that it is more natural for children to bury their parents. But we as parents do not expect to bury our children who have been healthy; we cringe at the thought.

We, whose thought patterns have been changed so quickly, almost in an instant, find it hard to believe others would not be thinking of death almost constantly. One can get the feeling of isolation in grief if the subject is ignored. One does not like to feel "apart" from others, but it is bound to happen if one cannot feel free to confide in others.

I believe others have no idea how much it is appreciated if they bear with the grieving in patience and understanding. The support of family and friends is so appreciated. It is very important to have someone to confide in that you can trust, even though it takes some sacrifice at times on the part of the trusted person. You never know how soon this role could be reversed and you could be the one who needs assistance. I thank God for the love of friends. One feels it when one is cushioned by the prayers of others. Did we become too dependent on it?

As time goes on, somehow you must find reasons to go on living. It is very important to do things you enjoy. Pursue a hobby. Even if you do not get much accomplished, at least it is a start. Start out with the little and simple things in life that often bring the most contentment: the robin returning in the spring; the catchy notes of the mockingbird; or the first buds appearing on a lilac bush, just to name a few.

Slowly, life starts anew. One could almost compare it to the cucifixion and then the resurrection of Jesus. After death, all hope for survival seems lost in a lonely and desolate world; then new hope springs forth after a period of time. Afterwards, you are not able to put your finger on the time when this really happened. It may take at least a year until you feel your energy returning. Then you may feel less tired. This happens gradually and you will not be able to pinpoint the exact time this physical healing actually started.

Faith, hope, and charity are three essentials in a Christian's life. The greatest of these three is love. Don't we all ask God for more love and more faith when we feel the need? But do we ever ask for more hope? If we ever come to a crisis in our lives when we feel life has no meaning, we need to dwell on thoughts of hope. Lack of hope disintegrates the mind. What is there to life without it? Life without hope is empty and meaningless; therefore, we cling to it in times of despair. We need to do that. It gives us a glimmer of light when all else has failed. Hope is a feeling that life and work have meaning after all, regardless of the conditions of the world surrounding us. It is a gift of God, filling our lives with the assurance of His nearness. We have learned to deeply depend on it, and it has not let us down.

*   *   *

In June, a good friend of ours who had also buried a child gave us a beautiful white rose bush, which means remembrance. My sister planted it for us by the gate in the front yard. All summer and until frost appeared there was always one white rose in bloom. What a beautiful memento! A year later as things sprang to life again, the rose bush was also greening.

Another memento: One day almost a year later, the UPS truck delivered a box which contained a blue spruce tree. One of my sisters sent it in remembrance of Junior. The boys took great pleasure and pride in keeping it watered. It came at an appropriate time—the day after Easter. The symbol of hope springing anew.

— Chapter 17 —

A Letter From Heaven

As the month of April arrived, we thought of our two missing children's birthdays. Johnnie's birthday was April 20, 1981. We never celebrate Jacob's birthday without thinking of his twin brother. Junior's birthday was also in April. As the day approached, our thoughts again drifted back to a year ago. How well I remembered his response when I asked if he would like to help bake a cake. He stirred the cake batter, and I told him it would be his birthday cake. That evening we lit the candles and sang, "Happy Birthday." His face beamed with pleasure.

Junior's birthday, April 23rd, arrived. It was not just a day of sadness, as some might think. Much more, it was a day of memories of things we liked to think about. We did not try to bury the past, neither did we dwell on it. We chose to cherish it because such memories brought us much joy amid the loneliness. A stranger from Rothsville stopped in that day. I had never seen her before. She said she had always wanted to stop by for a visit. She had also buried a son and April 23rd would have been his birthday. She wept as she said, "It's now nineteen years since my twenty-one-year-old son was killed, and I still miss him so much!" It is very common to have people express it that way, even after all those passing years. What a coincidence that it was also Junior's birthday.

We did receive a cake on that day. A close friend of mine came that afternoon with a box of ice cream and a beautiful cake decorated with white roses. On the cake was inscribed the words "Happy Birthday, Junior, Safe In the Arms of Jesus." As she gave me the cake and hugged me her eyes brimmed with tears and so did mine She knew she would weep if she did this, and she knew we would also, but that is the part we appreciated. Truly, tears cleanse the suffering soul. What a beautiful gesture of love this was in memory of Junior on that day. Before she left my friend gave me a letter and said we could read it after she left. We read the letter and it moved us to tears again and again. I still have to marvel at her ability to compose such a letter.

It read as follows:

A Note To My Family

Mother Dear, it's been some time now since I've seen your precious face and felt your loving arms around me. I do miss you, but Mother, I'm so happy here with Jesus. I know today is my birthday and you wish I was there with you all to celebrate this special day. But Mother, here in Heaven it is like having a birthday every day. Each moment here with Jesus is just so special. Nothing is comparable to having Jesus' arms around me and tenderly calling me his own child. The only thing that could make me possibly happier would be having you and Dad, Jacob, Samuel, Amos, and Emma here with me.

Oh, Mother, when I first came to live here, I saw the most precious little Angel. His smile was so bright and sunshiny and immediately I knew it was my brother Johnnie, who you had told me about. He came to show me his little angel wings, so beautiful! He's so happy here and was so glad to have me join this happy Angel Band. You know, Mother, I asked you all about the angels, and what we would do with our wings when we eat. Well, I need not have worried about little things like that, because Jesus has a perfect way to make all things work out.

Mother and Dad, I asked you so many things, questions about Heaven, when I was yet with you. But now, dear ones, everything is so easy to understand. And Mother and Dad, when you join me here, those things that now seem so hard to bear and hard to understand, those things will then seem as nothing, as you pass through those Heavenly Gates. Heaven is surely worth it all! Doesn't Heaven seem nearer since I am here? Mother, remember when we walked side-by-side and looked at the flowers and at our garden, and we thought they were so beautiful, and I just loved being near you? Those were happy times. But, dear ones, just wait till you see this Beautiful Garden here where Johnnie and I stroll through the streets of shining gold, hand-in-hand with Jesus and the other angels. What a sight to behold!

I'm so glad you taught me about Heaven and Jesus and His love for me. Because of that, I just felt at home in Heaven when Jesus bade me come. I'm glad for all those songs you taught me to sing and the Bible stories you read to me. Mother, I know you and Dad have shed many tears because you cannot see my face anymore, or feel my kisses on your cheeks, or hear my boyish voice saying, "I love you," or feel my warm hugs. But dear ones, it won't be long. Life on earth is only as a vapor. It won't be long till I stand at the door to welcome you and then we can be together forever.

Dad, I'll never forget the wonderful times we had when I followed you around as you did your work. I guess, then, I wanted to watch everything you did, so I could follow in your footsteps. But, dear Dad, Jesus had other plans for me and I answered His call, and now I snuggle upon His breast and lean my head on Him and feel His strong, protective arms encircle me. It reminds me of your love for me and the special times we spent together.

You and Mother did your very best to care for me and I want to thank you for this. But, dear ones, nothing within your power could have kept me there on earth with you when I heard Jesus calling me. He needed another rosebud to enhance the beauties of Heaven. And even though I knew you still wanted me, I had to go. It was such a wonderful unexplainable experience. Dad, someday you'll understand.

Brothers Jacob, Samuel, and Amos, remember those fun times we all had playing together? I loved each of you dearly and loved to share my time and things with you. It was so much fun romping together. It will be so wonderful when we can all be joined together, and just walk those fields of green clover, and talk, and all be wearing those snowy white angel wings.

The greatest joy of all is being here with Jesus. So, dear brothers, be obedient to Dad and Mother, and, most important of all, accept Jesus and live a life pleasing to Him so you are ready to join me here in this Happy Land. I love you, brothers, and want to see you again sometime. You will just love it, too!

I will close this letter—waiting—and watching for my loved ones to join me here in Gloryland. I love you, Mother, Dad, Jacob, Samuel, Amos, and little sister Emma. Johnnie, with his sweet angel voice, says, "Tell them all I love them, too."

With love, "Safe in the Arms of Jesus."

David, Jr.

It seemed I was able to get a glimpse into Heaven as I read that letter. I believe if we were actually allowed a glimpse into Heaven, our views in life would change. All the petty differences that arise among us humans would then seem so senseless.

The evening of Junior's birthday, Trooper Bittner treated us to supper. That was the finishing touch to a special day.

Chapter 18

One Year Later

Now, close to a year following Junior's death, I am still trying to grasp what happened. It seems awfully long since we saw his beautiful face! It is so hard to understand and it seems as if he could still come back to us. This thing of "trying to grasp it" is a feeling of when something is almost within reach, and when you can almost grasp it, it leaves you again and the struggle continues. I have come to the conclusion that the depth of such experiences and the mystery of death can never be fully understood by the human mind. It is too deep for us.

If we believe God **is** Sovereign and is in full control of our lives, then we must also believe God allows these happenings and has a purpose in them. He will not reveal His plans and purposes for our approval. We must not forget that He is God. I believe He wants us to believe and trust in Him in spite of the things we do not understand. If we cannot do this, we are destined to go through life with a weak, ineffectual faith, or no faith at all. By doing this we will just have to put our trust in some other foundation. But where? There really is no other foundation. We can read, "Except the Lord build the house, they labor in vain that build it." Psalm 127:1

I keep wondering how Junior would look now, a year later. Where would he fit in? As the boys go about their work and play, I wonder what he would be doing. I reflect on how it "had been;" not in sorrow, but in the many joys he gave us and all the good things he taught us.

The first week in May, I had a beautiful dream of Junior. In my dream, it was a beautiful, sunny, warm day. I looked out the window and saw Junior peacefully lying on the green grass taking a nap. A light breeze was gently blowing his white hair across his face. He was the picture of tranquil peace as he lay on his back, his arms thrown back, sound asleep. The dream was so vivid, I felt I could touch him. I awoke with tears on my pillow.

When school started in the fall, it seemed unbearably quiet. Little Emma seems to be almost a repeat of Junior. The older she gets, the more her personality reminds me of him. She is simply a bright spot in our lives and we tend to be very protective of her. She and I developed a daily conversation about Junior. She would ask me what Junior was doing, and I would tell her I didn't know. Then I would ponder aloud, "Junior, what are you doing? Are you singing or are you playing? Or are you picking pretty flowers? What **are** you doing?" Just pondering on those questions gave me intense longings to see him, and I would need to divert my thoughts to other subjects. Emma would ask me each day to repeat those same questions. If I wouldn't, then she would. Then she would say she wanted to see Junior, and I would tell her I thought she would some day.

*   *   *

It was Monday evening, and the date was May 24. As the day wore on, David and I felt keen memories of a year ago. It was now a year since Junior's death. We could relive almost every hour, every detail, and almost every minute of that same day as evening came. After supper David said he would like to work in the field and asked if I would finish the chores. I was, oh, so very tired with a tiredness that cannot be described! As I washed the milkers that evening, my mind wandered to a year ago. Vivid thoughts of Junior returned. Yes, even thoughts of the accident. As much as I wanted to avoid thinking of that painful scene, I still needed to face that, too, and learn to cope with it. I had learned that I could not cope by simply blocking out painful scenes or thoughts.

Before David left for the field he said to me, "Did you notice the time?" With that he left. I tried to sing, but the words stuck in my throat. Tears rolled silently down my cheeks. At 7:30 I felt I just needed to talk with someone who would understand, not to complain, but to express myself to someone. The jingling of the phone interrupted my thoughts. The caller was John Bramblett from Vermont. I asked, "How did you know when to call?" He said, "I know!" Yes, he did know. I was overwhelmed as I told him, "You caught me off guard. I seldom weep anymore, but tonight I had to." He said, "That's perfectly all right. I understand." We visited for half an hour. Again, I just marvelled at how our needs are met.

Months earlier we had read a book titled, *When Good-Bye is Forever.* It was written by someone who had buried two children over a period of several years. While reading it I felt I must meet this author some day because many of the thoughts I had written in my journal were almost identical to what I read in this book. Finally, by perseverance, I was able to contact the author. He and his wife and family lived in Vermont. In February they came to visit us, and that visit was one of the most memorable days in our lives.

Now just when I needed human contact with someone who cared, these friends from Vermont called. They related their feelings a year after their son, Christopher, was killed. Much of my weariness left because of their caring and sharing. We also received some nice cards and letters on that first anniversary of his death.

The next day was May 25th, the same date Junior was killed. I had a strong urge to know who the first person was to arrive at the scene of the accident. I was always troubled that I did not thank that man for what he did, and I was always afraid I had offended him by telling him, "Please, just let Junior go if he is not living any more." He said he was a fireman, and he was the one who gently administered artificial respiration resuscitation to Junior. Months earlier I had tried to contact this stranger but never succeeded. I did not know his name. Sometime during that day I decided to read the police report again, which was a fairly detailed report of what happened. While reading it I came to the statement written by Trooper Bittner when he was informed who the first person was to arrive at the scene, and there was the stranger's name! I knew it had to be that fireman whose name we did not know.

Now I knew what I needed to do. I was inspired to drop this stranger a note of thanks. After finding his address in the phone book, I wrote him a simple note of thanks and apologized if I had offended him. I also explained why I did not wish Junior to be disturbed if he had died, and told him about the child's desire to go to Heaven.

On Wednesday evening while I was washing the milkers, David brought a stranger to the door and asked me if I knew the man. I knew I had seen him before since he looked vaguely familiar. He told me he received my letter that day. I could see he had a problem keeping his emotions under control and so did I. He said he treasured the letter greatly—so seldom do they receive thanks. Theirs is mostly a "thankless job." This man said he felt so bad, fearing he had offended me by working on Junior when he felt I did not want him to. We all felt better then, and had a good visit. We asked him a lot of questions concerning Junior's death and his viewpoints on what he had observed. Another friend was added to our list.

As I reflect over the past year, I wonder how we survived. It was by the grace of a loving God and loving people. What seems most impressive to me is how it was possible to get our necessary work done, with the help of caring people, when our own strength had failed. Material things seemed so unimportant to us. In this day and age there is so much emphasis put on "things" instead of people. We focus on the importance of "things" while we could gain the greater blessing by focusing on the needs of people. Seeing or hearing anyone become upset over trivial or minor things only saddens me. In times of dire need, friends and neighbors came to our aid, and I could see so clearly how material and spiritual works go hand-in-hand, just as faith and works go hand-in-hand. If people would only have come and wished us well, that alone would not have done the work. It was the "fruits of the spirit" in action, for we could sense it was done in love. It was very touching and priceless. These were things that money could not buy.

I appreciate it even more now, in thinking of the unselfish generosity of people, of the hot meals, food, and bags of groceries brought to us. Small gifts for the children and bags of groceries were especially delightful to the children. I can find no words to adequately express our appreciation. The only way I can think of returning these kindnesses is by "passing it on." It reminds me of something I read years ago:

"Let the weakest, let the humblest remember, that in his daily course he can, if he will, shed around him almost a Heaven. Kindly words, sympathizing attentions, watchfulness against wounding men's sensitiveness—these cost very little, but they are priceless in value. Are they not almost staples of our daily happiness? From hour to hour, from moment to moment, we are supported, and blest by small kindnesses...." This is all very true.

David, Jr. will always be remembered by us as "the gentlest of flowers—a rare one." We try not to focus on the tragedy, but what we learned from it. As much as we would like to have him here with us, I thank God for taking Junior Home. We have not the heart to wish him back to this world we live in, after the Glory he has now! The thought of our two angels in Heaven is the most precious thought we could ever have. I am reminded of a verse in Zachariah: "And the streets in the city shall be full of boys and girls playing in the streets." Zachariah 8:5

When bedtime comes, I think of this verse:

Those dear little feet that pattered upstairs;
Each night at the setting of the sun.
Are pattering now the Golden Streets,
With Life's short journey done.

Chapter 19

The Boys Tell Their Stories In Their Own Words

Jacob's Story

The morning of Junior's accident, Mom and I had gone to a yard sale. There we saw a scooter and Mom bought it and we took it home. All day we boys took turns riding it.

After supper I made notes telling Junior, Sam, and Amos to go to the right place, go so and so far and get another note, and so on. The prize was the scooter. They finished the game I had made.

Then Sam and Junior started making one for me and Amos. While they were making it, me and Amos rode our scooters up the lane that goes between the road and the cornfield.

Suddenly we heard screeching of tires and a thump. We whirled around and saw Junior lying in the grass a few feet in front of the car.

I ran yelling for Mom and told her what had happened. She told me to tell Dad who was out in the end of the cornfield. I ran and told him. Together we went into the barn. Then Dad went to Junior. I went to the other side of the road against the barn with my brothers.

Some police cars pulled up. Some of the troopers began measuring skid marks, others went over to Junior. After a while two of them came up to us and asked us if we had seen what happened.

We told them what we had seen. They went down to their cars and got us each a teddy bear which they carry for such occasions. They didn't have one for Emma, so one trooper said he would get one for her. Later that evening he came back with a whole box of teddies and let Emma pick the one she wanted. She wanted a pink one.

While he was here, he talked with Aunt Rebecca who was with us while Dad and Mom were in the hospital.

The neighbors came over and said Dad had called them and told them to tell us Junior died. It was a shock. When we heard that, Rebecca, me, Sam, Amos, and Emma all went in to the couch.

After a while some people came. No one could sleep right that night. One thing I remember about Junior. He always seemed to be smiling. Some good things came out of this experience, such as learning to know different people.

Samuel's Story

I was in the tractor shed writing notes for the treasure hunt. I told Junior to take out one note to the mailbox. I looked to see if he had taken the one, but he hadn't. When he came back, I told him to take that note and get the other one, so he took it and went.

Suddenly I heard the tires screeching. I was very scared. Standing quickly, I looked out the open door. When I looked, I almost froze. There in the middle of the road was Junior and a speeding car was coming straight toward him. The car was going so fast it looked like a red streak, and I knew it could not stop. It was going way too fast. It hit Junior and stopped. I ran out of the shed, shaking all over. I looked over at the telephone pole and saw a red car and in the front was Junior, lying in the grass. The driver jumped out of the car and ran down to the barn yelling, "He's dead, he's dead!"

I ran over to Junior and saw him move his one eye and his lips were white and blue. Everything happened so quick it seemed like a fairy tale. Then Amos came running over, but I saw Jacob running out to Dad who was planting corn. I followed him out to Dad. At the end of the field I told them I think Junior's dead.

"How do you know he's dead?" Jacob asked.

"I just know he's dead," I said.

When we came in, Dad went to Junior and looked at him; then Amos and I went to the barn.

Later that evening the police came. We were standing near the barn. The policeman came and asked our names and ages. He had teddy bears for us, but he didn't have enough to give Emma one. At 9:00 another policeman came and gave a teddy bear to Emma. He talked with us and told us his name. That night it was impossible for any of us to sleep.

Amos's Story (age 7)

I heard the screeching of the tires of the car. I looked back and saw Junior lying on the grass, and I saw his hand move. I thought he was saying good-bye. Later a kind policeman came to us and put his arms around us.

— Chapter 20 —

My Husband Tells His Story

My first indication that anything was wrong was when I saw our three boys running toward me as I was planting corn. I saw Jacob fall flat and get up again as they all came running out as fast as they could. They were screaming and crying, "Junior has been hit by a car on the road, and he is dead!"

My first reaction was denial. "They probably don't know what they are saying" and, "It's not that bad." My next reaction was panic. My heart leaped to my throat and my mouth went dry. I thought of running wildly in to the road as the boys had run out. Then a deep sense of peace possessed me and an inner voice said, "Don't panic, everything is going to be all right."

In a daze, I continued toward the end of the field which leads to the barn. When I got to the end, I gave the reins to Jacob and told him to tie the horses to the barn.

I ran across the road to where Junior lay. There I met a man who said that Junior had a pulse, but he needed suction badly. He said, "Please talk to him and get him to respond." I took Junior's small hand in mine and called his name. No response. I called several more times. It seemed to me that he was breathing, but his breath was very shallow. I also noticed his one leg was broken. It bent not only at the knee, but between the knee and the ankle.

Another thing I noticed that I did not like was that his eyes were closed slightly, but they were not focused.

By this time I heard sirens in the distance. I figured as soon as the ambulance came, they would take him to the hospital and he would be taken care of. All in all, it was an almost peaceful scene.

Junior was lying on his back, with just a little bleeding out of his mouth and no moaning or crying. The stranger said he had a heartbeat.

By now more people arrived, plus a medic unit and an ambulance. They worked swiftly, cutting off his clothes and attaching a heart

76

monitor, then putting needles in his arms. After what seemed like a couple of minutes, I heard a low, urgent, "Let's go."

They put him on a stretcher and into the ambulance. I asked Esther if she wanted to go along with the ambulance. She said, "No, you go." I sat in the front seat in the ambulance. The driver was a person we knew. He had often jogged past our place.

On the way in the lights flashed and the sirens sounded, while cars pulled off the road. I could not see Junior or hear very much. Once I heard someone say, "It's not a cardiac arrest, but the next thing to it." Being in a daze and still believing that everything would be all right, I did not fully comprehend what I heard. Yes, I did think there was a possibility that he might not live. It was a fleeting thought.

When we got to the hospital a lady whom I presumed to be a doctor came with a medic unit. She took me aside and told me, "I just want to warn you. It doesn't look good."

After a while the hospital chaplain came and introduced himself to me and took me to the Family Consultation Room. He said he would be back later to tell me how they were making out with Junior. Now I was sitting alone in the room. A picture of Jesus was on the wall, a Holy Bible lay on the small stand, and several Bible verses were on the wall. I suddenly thought, "What am I doing here? Why am I in here?" Being in a daze, I could not think clearly.

Later Esther and her parents came, and my parents came also. Soon the doctor came and said Junior was hurt very badly; they needed more tests and x-rays. He told us he would be back later.

When he came back, he quietly said, "Even though your son's heart is still beating by itself, he is brain dead." He told us we had a choice of either keeping him on a life support machine or taking him off. I asked him what he would do if this was his child, and the doctor said he would take him off since there was no hope that he would ever recover. If they took Junior off the machine, it would be only a matter of time until the heart would stop by itself.

The doctor asked if we would like to see Junior, and we said we would. Someone took us down the hall, and reality struck. There he was. Two nurses were with him; one was squeezing a bulb which was breathing for Junior, and there were tubes attached to him. I looked at my youngest son, who was lying very still, and silently said, "Good night."

We went back to the consultation room where we met Dr. Argires.

When he told us that Junior had been killed instantly, I asked why his heart was still beating. The doctor explained that a young child's heart can continue to beat for twenty or thirty minutes after his death. He said Junior had a brain stem injury. When the car hit him, his head was above the hood of the car. The impact was so great that it stretched his vertebras, causing the brain stem to swell up and shut off the blood supply to his brain, which caused his death. He also had extensive internal injuries.

The doctors asked if we would be willing to donate Junior's organs. We could help someone to have a better life. Was this the reason he had to be brought in here? We could not view the whole thing in our own eyes. The decision was not hard for me to make, but Esther was more hesitant and agreed to abide by my decision.

We thought about an eighteen-year-old boy who had a liver transplant only the week before. We also thought about our cousin who had a kidney transplant years ago. Someone had donated their organs to him; were we going to accept them and not be willing to give in return? We were also reminded of my father-in-law, who had years of pain in his eye until he received another cornea. We knew how much better his life was after he received another cornea; he was sitting there in the room with us. With these thoughts in mind, we consented. Dr. Argires looked at us with tears in his eyes and said, "It is the most unselfish thing you could have done." However, upon examination only one kidney was useful. All the other organs were damaged by the impact, and he had many broken bones. The doctor told us that if Junior had lived he would never have been normal.

I believe Junior suffered very little compared to what he would have suffered had he survived. In another perspective, had he lived and returned to normal he probably would have done a lot of good on this earth. Why it happened this way is beyond my understanding.

"Not my will be done, but thine."

How gladly we would have kept him with us yet, but it was not to be.

When we came home from the hospital, friends and neighbors had gathered at our house. Many tears were shed; many prayers were offered; many encouraging words were shared.

Our dear son's burial was two days later at Upper Millcreek Cemetery, where we viewed him for the last time on this earth. How sad I felt! I bade him a final farewell and whispered, "Good night," yet we look forward to meeting him in Heaven. The feeling was much the same as our parting with our son Johnnie. Meanwhile, we had to somehow go on living, however hard it was.

A few days after Junior's funeral I was up in the barn, watching the rain outside. It was very dismal weather for a grieving person. I was so very tired. As I sat there my thoughts were, "Why did a car have to come just then? Why did he need to be killed?" Just then I saw a little bird land on the telephone wire. As I watched, I saw the little bird suddenly fall to the road. I wondered, "Will this little bird also get hit?" Then zoom, a car came and drove over the bird, killing it instantly. My mind was jolted! Now why did that little bird live, only to die so young? Didn't God care? Even while thinking that question, I knew in my heart that God does care. He cares a lot.

"Are not two sparrows sold for a farthing? And one of them shall not fall to the ground without your Father knowing it. But the very hairs of your head are numbered. Fear ye not therefore. Ye are of more value than many sparrows." Matthew 10:29-31

Also, I am reminded that God thinks and works differently than we do. "For My thoughts are not your thoughts, neither are My ways your ways, saith the Lord. For as the Heavens are higher than the earth, so are My ways higher than your ways, and My thoughts than your thoughts." Isaiah 55:8-9

I am also reminded of Job. "And the Lord said unto Satan, Has thou considered My servant Job? There is none like him in the earth, a perfect and upright man; one that feareth God and escheweth evil?" Job 1:8. Here was a man worth a lot of money, who owned lots of sheep, camels, oxen, and asses. He also had seven sons and three daughters, and these were all taken from him in one day. What a blow! Yet he did not curse God, but said, "Naked have I come out of my mother's womb and naked shall I return thither. The Lord gave and the Lord hath taken away; blessed be the name of the Lord." Job 1:21

What a comfort that story is to me. Certainly I do not put myself on the same level as Job, but his faith is an inspiration to me. How much less reason do I have to lose faith in God compared to Job? He did not lose faith despite his trials, and neither should I. It still rains at times and things seem as dismal as before, but I am reminded that God is still in control and there was a purpose in the life and death of Junior.

He was a sunshiny boy. We had nicknamed him "Bubbs," for as a toddler he had bubbled over with sunshine. He had blond hair and big blue eyes, with pink cheeks and a ready trusting smile, yet he had a seriousness beyond his years.

I believe that God could have prevented this accident from happening, but God in His wisdom let Junior die in a manner totally different than was his nature. A very gentle person was killed in such an ungentle way.

Did I need to be reminded of something? Was Junior's life and death an inspiration to someone he knew? Was it an inspiration to someone he didn't know? Perhaps all of the above and even more beyond my field of view. My knowledge is so limited I cannot answer my own questions. We need to look up, to lean on a higher power, the Lord God Almighty.

Chapter 21

TROOPER BITTNER SHARES HIS STORY

Preface

When I was asked to compose this manuscript, I could not begin to imagine where I would begin. I have made a career of reporting facts and events. Just the way they happen—no more or less. But now I was asked to put my point of view, feelings, impressions, and opinions on paper. It frightened and intimidated me, but as I thought about it, I saw healing.

I do not remember exact dates or times; names at times escape me. But the events of one single day have changed my life forever. It has shaped who and what I am forever.

Prelude

It was like any other morning. The dew was heavy on the grass and soaked through my boots as I walked my dog, Bear. Dawn assaulted the darkness and drove off the chill of this spring morning. My shift for the day started at 3:00 p.m. My shift the previous night ended at 11:00 p.m., so I was glad for some time by myself this morning. At 2:00 I swallowed the last of my coffee and started for the station. The night before had been predictably slow. Ephrata Station was not known for many notable incidents, and today held the promise of neighbor complaints, stray dogs, and traffic violators.

As I crossed East Brubaker Valley Road, the farm on the bend near the mid-point of that road caught my eye. The sun played on the freshly plowed fields and whitewashed buildings and gave a tremendous pastoral sense as I went to my unpredictable shift, not knowing what the next eight hours would bring. As the road unfolded in front of me, I passed the farm and my thoughts focused on a game plan for the day.

When I arrived at the station Corporal Ramos, the shift supervisor, had roll call. Nothing of note had happened overnight, and he gave the option of patrol zones. Since Marty Zeamer had a trainee with him, I gave him the first choice. Trooper Fred Hess needed experience, so he chose the east zones, which had the 222 bypass and a reputation for being more active. That left me with the west: farmlands and State Game Lands. Slow day on tap. I didn't mind. I poured a cup of coffee and sat down at a desk to log my citations from the night before.

By 3:30 p.m. I was on the road. The first order of business was to swing through and clear my zones. In doing this I would drive the major roads, checking for abandoned vehicles or traffic hazards. In general, I was letting the public know that "the State" was on the road. As I drove through the game lands, I marvelled at the rebirth that was taking place. The dogwoods were blooming; grass was greening; a plowed field was steaming as the sun was approaching mid-day. I picked up Route 322 in Brickerville, just east of Route 501. As I approached the light, a grey sedan crossed in front of me as the light turned green. For general purposes, I stopped the car. The driver offered no excuse. I gave him a written warning and advised him to slow down and pay attention. I couldn't help but wonder if he would listen. I decided, probably not.

By 5:30, I was being reminded of not having eaten lunch. I called the station to get permission to go for dinner. Joan Keller, the Police Communications Operator, or PCO, asked the Corporal and I got the okay. It was a slow day and I would be at the edge of my zones. My thoughts were that I could spend a half hour with Bear over dinner. He loved to play when he didn't expect me. When I showed up I caught him on the sofa, dozing. I softly scolded him, made a sandwich, and headed outside. He romped while I ate. I decided my life was good. As I finished my sandwich, I put Bear back inside, ruffled his ears, and headed for the car. I heard the PCO on the radio, calling Zeamer and Trooper Hess by car number.

The Accident

"Ephrata to Ephrata-2."

"Ephrata 2-Bye."

"10-45, East Brubaker Valley Road, west of Hammercreek Road. Pedestrian, code 2."

"Ephrata-2, where's Bittner?"

"Ephrata, Ephrata-2, he's at lunch. 10-6."

"10-4 10-17."

Well, I was done. It was my zone; Marty had a trainee, so he couldn't do it.

"Ephrata-5 to Ephrata."

"Go ahead Ephrata-5."

"I'm 10-24, I'll handle 10-17."

"2 to 5, you sure?"

"10-4 please assist."

"10-4 E.T.A. 10 minutes."

They would get there before me. I was seven minutes at code 2, so they could secure the scene and appraise me when I got there.

As I tapped the switch for the overhead lights, the engine sprang to life. All my senses sharpened, alert for other drivers. The lights and siren often made people do unpredictable things. Coming down East Brubaker Valley Road, I could see the lights from the ambulance at the scene. I realized my siren was still on, so I cut it off. The fire official at the intersection of Sleepy Hollow Road was waving me through, his arms flailing like a windmill.

I put on my hat. I knew the routine. Time now to earn my pay. Zeamer was parked on the south side, by the barn. An ambulance was on the north side, just beyond the drive for the house, in front of a red car. I could see the skid marks leading to the car and knew what had happened. My mouth went dry, and my throat got tight. I gained my composure and stepped out of my car. Zeamer walked up to me as I asked, "What have we got?"

His face grim, he flatly said, "One car. Hit a child crossing the road. It doesn't look good." He told me the driver was shaken and sitting in the back of his car.

As accidents go, this one was nothing out of the ordinary on the surface. I went about collecting the necessary information for the report, taking measurements and photos. Zeamer came to me and said he had interviewed the children. As he talked I looked to the barn, where the children were standing, lined up by size. With that sight, the impact this one event would have on the Smuckers began to set in. The children stood alone, quietly sobbing, not quite knowing exactly what had happened to their brother.

I took a deep breath. The sun was beginning to slip into the western sky, and the shadows were growing long. I noticed the cameraman from News 8 in the middle of the accident scene and asked him to clear out until we were finished. I began to summarize all the information I had collected, to make sure I had everything. The driver of the car, had been put in the back of my patrol car. He was to go to the hospital to have his blood checked for alcohol. This was standard procedure in the case of serious or fatal accidents. I checked on him and let him know we would soon be going. His tear-stained face looked at me as he broke into open weeping.

As I closed the car door, an Amish woman approached me. She seemed small, her face was pale, her eyes pleading. From her clothes, I could tell she had left chores undone. A small Amish girl, her daughter, clung to the hem of her dress. I turned to face her. She carried her hands, folded on her chest, as if she were praying. As she stopped, closer to me than I normally would allow someone, she opened her mouth as if to say something, paused, then said, "Please take care of the boy." I assumed she meant the boy who had been hit, her youngest son. I replied, "The ambulance and doctors will do everything they can. The rest is up to God."

She looked to the back seat of my car and said, "I mean the driver. We forgive him."

I simply told her I would remember that. Then I politely excused myself, got into the patrol car, and started for the hospital. The ride to the hospital took only twenty minutes. The young lad questioned me as to what would become of him. I explained how the legal system worked, and how at the very least, he would get a citation or "ticket." Questions of his own morality and God's plan for him tumbled from him like water over a dam about to burst. This gave me the opportunity to witness about God and His plan for all of us.

As we talked, he began to calm down. I learned that his father was a minister. I thought he must think it strange that I was witnessing to him, yet the voice of God spoke in me, "Have faith and trust Me." I let the Spirit take over. I found answers and wisdom and believe that it was God speaking through me. What a wonderful blessing to feel the Spirit above in one's life! As I was soon to discover, this was not the last time.

The Hospital

We arrived at the hospital to find the usual rush of emergencies, doctors, nurses, and a myriad of people in crises.

We entered the Emergency Room. I explained to the head nurse what we needed. I saw the Smuckers, David and Esther, in the doctor's office. They looked very tired. I looked back to my charge and saw him staring. I followed his gaze. The curtain for one of the beds was slightly parted. There, looking very small, was David, Junior. The noise about me grew distant. I saw a tear roll down the observer's cheek. I stepped between him and the opening and went to be with Junior, closing the curtain. The technicians were busy trying to maintain his life. I asked what his chances were. A male nurse said, "He's brain dead. It's up to his parents." I looked down at his small face. I saw my own son.

I had been divorced years before, and my son now lived with his mother over 250 miles away. The anger between his mother and me had kept me from him for three years. He was four years old, and I hardly knew him.

Without a word I turned, walking with the weight of the world on my shoulders. The Smuckers came out of the doctor's office and went to where Junior lay. I spoke to the doctor who told me they had decided not to keep Junior on life support. Okay. Now I knew the heading for the report. I told the young driver of the car to sit tight.

After entering the employees' rest room and locking the door behind me, I looked at myself in the mirror. I stand six feet tall and the campaign hat makes me even taller, hiding my eyes beneath the brim. Looking closer, I saw the chin strap resting on my lower lip almost made me look like I was smiling. It hid my tightly drawn lips. I took off that hat for the first time since beginning the investigation almost five hours before. For the first time in my career, I reacted emotionally to an investigation. Merely allowing the first tears to roll brought more. I cried, as my body shook with sorrow. Not only did I cry for the Smuckers and the driver who hit Junior, but also for myself.

I knelt on one knee, folded my hands, and prayed, "Lord, this is beyond me. All power and glory is Yours. For too long I have lived a life for me, calling on You when things get tough. I give my life to You now. All I do is to Your glory. Make me an instrument of Your mighty plan, that my words and deeds might magnify You! This I pray in Jesus' name. Amen."

The tears subsided. I washed my hands and face, straightened my tie, and put the hat back on my head. My steps quicker and lighter, I stepped out.

The Learning

In the weeks following the accident, patrol in the Smuckers' area held new meaning. It was determined that speed inforcement was needed on East Brubaker Valley Road. Many motorists bought a share of the Commonwealth in the months that followed.

As I would sit in their drive or by the barn, the Smuckers would stop and talk. The children would stand by their parents, quietly, and listen. One day after the investigation was closed and I had told them, Esther told me she had something for me, but she did not know if it was proper. I told her it would be all right. It was fresh bread.

As time passed, I went through a great deal of uncertainty. I had done my job, reporting and policing, yet I felt a closeness with this family. Why? Why were they so kind to me? It is not a good practice to become involved with those whose lives have been so deeply touched. My purpose was to protect and serve, not to get personally involved. It is taught in the academy and preached in the field.

I prayed for wisdom and guidance. The Lord is ever faithful.

I opened myself to this family and found a gift more precious than diamonds!

Esther would share her feelings with me. When I would patrol there, the kids would run out to meet me. David always had a warm smile and a hearty handshake, saying, "Well, hello there, Bill."

My family had fallen apart before I became a state trooper. To this point, the cold autonomy of professionalism had ruled my life. Now, this family had "adopted" me. David and Esther were like my siblings. The children, almost as if they were my own. Still, in quiet moments I was uneasy. As I prayed for understanding, it did not come. Some days I would not go home past that farm.

Then one day my pager sounded. It was the barracks. The news of another accident almost brought me to my knees. Jacob, the oldest, had fallen from a piece of farm equipment on to the top of a passing car. He was at the hospital. Arriving at the farm, I found Esther in the milkhouse, trying to be brave. I thought my heart would break. She told me David had gone in with the ambulance; she had to see that the chores got done. "Nonsense!," I said. The neighbors would feed and milk the cows. She would go with me to the hospital to get David. I tried to reassure her that Jacob would be fine.

On the way to the hospital we prayed and shared silence. When we got there, David's parents and Esther's sister met us. Going back to see Jacob was like....

He was fine. A bump on the head, some bruises, but fine. He would stay overnight to be monitored. I dropped David and Esther at their home. In the silence as I made my way home, God spoke to me. "My son, your son."

"THAT'S IT!" John, my son!

I sang a prayer of thanks and found ways to begin to know my son. I called him that weekend. We made plans to see my dad, and to begin again.

Truly, God is faithful! No lamb does He allow to stray. With gentleness, He will lead the lost back to the flock of their own accord.

Not The End

My career has taken me away from that stretch of East Brubaker Valley Road. I live in this fast-paced, modern world. I have been given additional responsibilities, and my time is taxed to the point of frustration. My life has become so busy it seems I can't keep up. I need a reminder to slow me down. Then I receive a card or short note from the Smuckers. It never fails to get my thoughts in the right perspective again. A close walk with God. Sometimes I find a loaf of bread and preserves on my doorstep, with a note "Guess Who?"

David, Esther, Jacob, Samuel, Amos, and dear, sweet Emma. Their faith and love have given my life purpose. They have allowed me to feel again. Most importantly, they have given this father his son, and this son back to his Father. That is our God!

"Oh, Heavenly Father, Master of all mysteries and giver of all Life; I thank You and praise You. Your loving kindness and wisdom does shine as a beacon unto those of us lost on seas of worldliness. It is through Your Son, Jesus Christ, that all may one day return to You. It was by His death on the cross that Your promise of Everlasting Life is secured. I turn my eyes to Heaven, and believe that this is the beginning. All Glory is yours, Lord God Almighty! In Jesus' name, Amen."

THANK YOU, GOD

Thank you so much for lending us
Just for a little while,
Two twining arms,
A trusting tilted chin
A dimple in the middle.
(You know, Lord, for You made him.)

Eyes as blue as clearest summer skies;
The utter frankness of his knowing grin. Thanks!
Thanks so much
For allowing us to clutch for one short space
His little hand in ours.

We've put away his little coat,
(You'll keep him warm)
His little shoes,
(He has no need for them on Heaven's meadows)
His slightly grimy teddy bear,
(No need for happy pastime over there)
All but the memory of happy,
Carefree, love-rich summer days

And humbly, thank you God
That 'neath a shroud of sorrow,
Despite stark grief and throbbing pain
You taught us how to praise
And thank you, thank you again,
For sending once your Son to die for us
That we, without a hint of dread,
Could give you back
Our little son.

Reprinted with permission from
Five Loaves and Two Small Fishes by Margaret Penner Toews.